"Harrowing to read, but ultimately healing and filled with hope. Even in the darkest times of our lives, God never lets go."

—**Francine Rivers**, author

"As an experienced therapist, I cannot recommend this book more highly as support and encouragement for those struggling to follow Jesus—whatever their circumstances. Leigh offers specific tools, strategies, and biblical references for helping your clients of faith. May you be blessed by the reading of Leigh's words—profound nuggets and powerful scriptures combined with candor and compassion."

—**Dr. Michele Novotni**, PhD, coauthor of *Angry with God*

"As someone who works with traumatized children and their families, I believe Leigh's bravery in honestly sharing the painful journey toward healing will serve as a beacon to many grappling with traumatic histories. Equally important, her clear testimony that a deep and abiding faith doesn't necessarily make the journey easy but does make it possible is a message that so many need to hear. As promised in Philippians 4:13, we CAN do all things through Christ who strengthens us. Leigh is living proof of that, and her book is a gift to all those struggling to find a path forward, as well as to those who love and support them on the journey."

—**Dr. Debbie Reed**, PhD, president/CEO of Chaddock (https://www.chaddock.org/)

"Leigh's captivating story is a powerful example of how EMDR therapy can help the mind and body process traumatic events in order to reconcile past trauma. As in Leigh's story, EMDR can lead us to a deep 'mind-body-spirit' healing. I plan to use her book as a resource to support other trauma survivors through their journey, to help instill a message of hope for healing, and as a testimony to the healing that can occur with EMDR. It is also important to note that *faith* can be a powerful tool in recovery and can be paired with EMDR or any modality to heal from the past. Leigh's story is a perfect example of this."

—**Tara Krueger**, LCSW / CCTP II

"As a psychologist who specializes in therapy for traumatized children and adults, I found Leigh's descriptions of the lessons she learned so sound and practical that I will be recommending her book to my clients as a companion for my therapy work. The Bible verses she shares caused me to learn and see things in Scripture I had not recognized before now. This was refreshing in itself. I cannot say enough about the psychological, emotional, and spiritual credibility of this book. Please read it! Read it for yourself or for the person you love who has been through traumatic experiences that wounded them. Read it to educate yourself if you have not experienced trauma. Just read it!"

—**Cara R. Johnson**, MSW, PsyD, Missouri licensed psychologist

"We are all broken at some level, needing to be fought for and then to fight for others. Leigh Mackenzie chronicles her brokenness and the battles she fought by herself and alongside others in *She Seems So Normal*. Let Leigh help you fight as she pulls back the veil on her struggles, revealing the small and great victories that can be won through Christ and His people."

—**Jerry Harris**, publisher, Christian Standard Media; teaching pastor, The Crossing Church

"The healing hope of Leigh Mackenzie is contagious in every way. So many trauma survivors carry around an invisible weight that is rarely seen. With brave and beautiful boldness, Leigh's vulnerability lets us see her story of how she found new freedom in Jesus. *She Seems So Normal* is a powerful memoir providing a compass to anyone looking for real transformation."

—**Jeanne Stevens**, founding lead pastor of Soul City Church; author of *What's Here Now?*

"To be human, someone said, is to be in trouble. We fallen creatures face brokenness in our lives and in our world, but too rarely do we square up to look it in the eye. My dear friend Leigh Mackenzie does just that in this riveting and encouraging book. She bares her soul and tells her story in a way that helps us to see the brokenness in our world. But she also helps us to choose to face our own brokenness, to seek the Lord and enlist the help of others, and to push through the darkness to see the light. Read this book. Give it to a fellow struggler. Face your own brokenness with faith. God's grace is available; Leigh's story is a glorious testimony to this fact."

—**Alvin Reid**, PhD, author of *Sharing Jesus {Without Freaking Out}*

"In a world where survivors are often silenced, Leigh Mackenzie bravely stands up to proclaim that her voice will be heard. Her raw vulnerability shines a light on the truth that every story matters, even when those stories feel too messy or painful to share. Revealing the mysteries behind true healing, *She Seems So Normal* offers all survivors hope for a better tomorrow."

—**Ciji Wagner**, founder of Louder Than Silence

"In excruciating honesty, Leigh Mackenzie exposes the deception of perfectionism in the body of Christ that threatens to rob the American church of the authentic, inexhaustible power of the gospel to transform our broken souls into the wholeness Jesus lives to give. This work is profound."

—**Eulalia King**, award-winning Christan songwriter, Lifeway Bible study contributor

"Leigh Mackenzie is a courageous and energetic writer with a personal story of shattering and redemption. *She Seems So Normal* pulses with raw honesty and unrelenting hope. This book is a brain changer for anyone dragged down by past pain, shame, and trauma."

—**Randy Petersen**, coauthor of *The One-Year Book of Women in Christian History*

"Leigh Mackenzie's gut-level honesty about her struggles knows no bounds because she cares deeply for your soul. This book is God-breathed through the fingers of this amazing woman of God. Leigh Mackenzie has received healing for her broken life. Now let her help you find yours."

—**Dr. Jamie Morgan**, mentor to women in ministry, TrailblazerMentoring.com

"*She Seems So Normal* is a story of death and resurrection. With enormous courage, candor, and grace, Leigh Mackenzie offers readers a rare first-person account of life in the unquenchable hell of child sexual abuse and her struggle to escape its fiery pit. Her powerful words show us how Jesus provides a path toward healing. This book is a must-read for anyone who is suffering from the soul-searing torment of child sexual abuse and those who accompany them."

—**Martha Brune Rapp**, DMin, Roman Catholic
lay minister, certified spiritual director, and author
of *Conversations with Benjamin*

"*She Seems So Normal* is a culmination of prayer, counseling, therapy, and many lunches together! Leigh tells her story with grace, humor, and strength. As a pastor's wife, I think *She Seems So Normal* is a phrase to embrace, a prayer to pray, and an awesome book to read!"

—**Allison Harris**, The Crossing Church

"With extreme honesty, clarity, and humility, *She Seems So Normal* is profoundly relatable. Leigh vulnerably ends the narrative by wrapping up God's healing power and restoration in a ribbon of love. There is RESOLUTION! Childhood demons were addressed openly, honestly, and vanquished! So many need this."

—**Karen Dennis**, pastor's wife, leader/mentor
for reGeneration

"I want to thank you for your podcast. It's helped me in many ways I can't even explain in words right now. But it's helped me to start to move from being stuck and defeated to, I have no clue, but it's better. I just know that. My story is similar to yours. Thank you for being brave, for learning and growing, and for sharing all that you do; it's quite helpful and a safe spot to listen to someone who is further along on this journey to healing."

—podcast listener

SHE SEEMS SO NORMAL

Shatter
the
Plastic
Princess,
Embrace
Authentic
Faith

LEIGH MACKENZIE

BROOKSTONE
PUBLISHING GROUP
Birmingham, Alabama

She Seems So Normal

Brookstone Publishing Group
An imprint of Iron Stream Media
100 Missionary Ridge
Birmingham, AL 35242
IronStreamMedia.com

Library of Congress Control Number: 2022909998

Cover design by twoline || Studio

ISBN: 978-1-949856-69-9 (paperback)
ISBN: 978-1-949856-70-5 (e-book)

1 2 3 4 5—27 26 25 24 23

To Christopher, Jug, and Blu—my champions,
my family, my heart.

To Old Ox—we plowed the pain of the 23rd together.
Thank you for never giving up on me.

The LORD is my shepherd,
I shall not want.
He makes me lie down in green pastures;
He leads me beside quiet waters.
He restores my soul;
He guides me in paths of righteousness
For His name's sake.
Even though I walk through the valley
of the shadow of death,
I fear no evil, for You are with me;
Your rod and Your staff, they comfort me.

—Psalm 23:1–4 (NASB 1995)

Death above and death below, I find my run has taken me through this valley of shadow as a snapshot of what's to come. Unearthing scattered, dishonored, and decades-abandoned skeletons from the past, can I order them with the respect, care, and love they deserve?

Who gets to know the ending to their journey before it begins?

I guess right now, I do.

CONTENTS

ACKNOWLEDGMENTS

Eighteen years ago, my persistent friend Amy Beck asked me to Bible study *seven* times before I reluctantly said yes to going to Jill Shoot's home for coffee and Jesus. We knew each other when we were worms and now look how far the Lord has brought us.

Tara Krueger (LCSW and EMDR therapist), my apologies for being bossy, defensive, and controlling in our first session. You may never know how much it meant to me that you watched over me through the Red Room and all the other pits of hell . . . and made me go back until we conquered them.

Amanda & 929 worship team and peeps, through therapy, you allowed me to discover my voice again, to harmonize while healing, and to serve the higher calling of praising God instead of remaining trapped in my darkest moments. #929Proud

My IG ladies: Delphine Kirkland, Wilma Hollis, Robin Wisner, Betsy Pendergrass (and so many others too numerous to name), you were my people, my prayer warriors. Judy Dunagan and Tina Smith, you taught me a ton and equipped me for this season of spiritual warfare. Prayer Warrior Peter (and post-manuscript, Karen Hetzler), you helped me IRT at the end to birth the ministry and give me confirmation of the message.

5AM Fabi and Team Turtle (Chantal and Jess), you galvanized and fast-tracked this project. Team Turtle and Holly M encouraged me after every podcast episode released that people needed this message and I was on the right track, even sharing the podcast with friends around the world and Chicago Uber drivers along the way.

Ciji Wagner, thank you for just "getting" me so I didn't have to explain my trauma-crazy. Your work at Louder Than Silence to support other sexual assault survivors in Cohorts and to help them get the EMDR therapy they need means so much to me. I'm thrilled to partner with LTS and offer a portion of the proceeds from this book to help you help others like us.

Dr. John "Big Fish" Herring of Iron Stream Media and Brookstone Creative Group, who, alongside Michele Trumble, championed this book to publication, thank you for seeing my vision for the #ShowYourCrown movement and for hearing my heart's cry for authentic transparency (and also for agreeing to the QR Codes!). I'm grateful to Dr. Katherine Hutchinson-Hayes for a first run at the edits that became part 3 of the book.

Dr. Alvin Reid, we did the hard stuff piecing together the memories through that content edit, didn't we? You gave me structure for the manuscript and grace in the story along with remarkable direction and a few rockin' transitions. Thanks for having the courage to serve our audience through an incredibly difficult narrative to produce a cohesive story.

Senior editor Susan Cornell and copy editor Karissa Silvers: what would I have done without all your dangling modifier fixing, verb tense changing, and fact double-checking? Your talents bless both me and the reader.

In the "clean-up" phase, there's still more work to heal a lifetime of negative patterns and PTSD. The tandem support of my current dynamic duo—Northwestern Medicine's trauma therapist Ron Migalski, LCSW, and psychiatrist Dr. Allen Georges—has been yet another game changer.

Allison Harris, thank you for the opportunity to begin professionally writing and delving into Scripture in earnest, for advocating for me to assist with sermon and illustration ideas for Jerry. Thank you BOTH for giving this ol' horse a shot. You suggested I document my journey, Allison, prayed me through some pretty jacked up spiritual attacks, and drank a lot of coffee and tea with me as I processed, so this is all your fault.

My Old Ox, Dr. Michele Novotni (and super-husband Bob!): thank you for not giving up on me, even when I was thinking your thoughts for you and sabotaging our friendship every way I knew how. We have plowed a far row together, haven't we? There aren't enough words to express this Young Ox's love and gratitude for your wisdom and prayers.

Christopher, Julian, and Bella, you are my champions. I love you. (You know I can't write any more without writing a novel or dissolving into tears!)

Jesus, Jesus . . . You make the darkness tremble and silence fear. Thank You for walking with me through the deepest brimstone pits of the valley and never leaving my side, even when I didn't know You were there. You are the hero of every believer's story.

For all the trauma survivors and the people who love and support them, the King of kings sees your struggle, Jesus knows your pain, and the Holy Spirit and the Church beckon you in a "divine duet," Come. "Let him who hears say, 'Come!' Whoever is thirsty, let him come" (Revelation 22:17 NIV84TPT).

For survivor support or to donate to
Louder Than Silence

READER NOTE

Crowns: Throughout *She Seems So Normal* you'll see crown symbols in the margin (like the one here) accompanied by a number indicating a short podcast episode of me reading and possibly reflecting on that section of the work. The QR code for the podcast will be at the end of each chapter. Scan the code and then select whichever episode you want. Please feel free to share episodes with others as the Lord leads.

QR Codes: Occasionally, you will also see QR codes at the ends of chapters to access the various resources cited. They will also be accompanied by the actual website addresses in the notes section at the back of the book.

She Seems So Normal podcast

THE SHATTERING

As I measured the stone's weight in my chubby six-year-old palm, my fingers caressed its smooth surface. *This'll do.*

The rock warmed to match the temperature of the fury boiling in my veins. Picking my target, I gritted my teeth and set my jaw. Gripping the rock close to my ear, I stepped forward and hurled it with every ounce of raw emotion housed in my soul.

Suddenly the world skidded into slow motion. The high-pitched sound came first, probably because I had squeezed my eyelids shut to muster my strength and focus. I opened my eyes wide to watch the old farmhouse window coming down in shards, multiple pieces breaking at the point of impact. The sunlight glinted off every beautiful facet; I was delighted and proud of my grand spectacle, infused with the energy of the rhapsody I created until my family ran out, shouting, "What happened?"

What had I done? The wreckage gave witness to my wrath and right where I stood, the Colorado sun shone like a stage spotlight with me as its focus. With her mouth agape, hands up and open in surrender—or perhaps as if she could stop the last dangling pieces from hitting the hard ground—my mother looked at me with daggers in her eyes as she spoke.

"What have you done?"

Suddenly, my rage became fear.

It was a naughty thing, and I knew it. I knew I would be in trouble, but I don't think I cared. That day I exercised some of my tiny power while hoping to exorcise some demons terrorizing my young mind. This proved so exhilarating that in every house after that, broken windows, kicked-in doors, and walls riddled with punch holes stood as witnesses to my anger. The fury raging inside Little Me built over time since I lacked positive methods for venting big emotions. I was a child helpless to act against those who hurt me, and the anger grew with me through my adolescence into womanhood and awkwardly tumbled out sideways at the most inopportune times in ever-increasing, shameful ways.

Rocks through windows were the best way I could cope as a child. Later, self-doubt, self-hate, sabotaging behaviors, people-pleasing, anorexia, bulimia, drinking, acting out, and risk-taking behavior all became coping mechanisms in my struggle. Oh, and rugby . . . yes, rugby, a sport where I literally got tackled on the field and relished my chance to hit back. Physically, I was painfully broken or massively bruised after most games, so my theme remained the same: I would somehow always pay the price.

I ask myself now, *Why windows?* I believe a deeper meaning hides in layers behind the glass. Glass is delicate and strong at the same time. Windows keep out rain and snow and stand up to all kinds of winds and weather, but they shatter when hit at the right place. Pyrex glass withstands freezing and microwaving, but put it over a direct flame, and it cracks and breaks. You can heat or cool tempered glass bowls, but even they shatter with any extreme temperature change, like when setting a hot one on a cool countertop.

Ever dropped a wine glass? Its shattering makes a crazy mess. Even after you thoroughly clean, sweep, and mop, you find broken pieces everywhere in unexpected places.

Shattering a child with trauma is the same.[1]

Sometimes the safest place to face challenging subjects is between a book's covers. Within these pages you'll read the raw, honest story of a believer who's been as close as she could get to hell and back. I'm no expert on mental health or trauma but simply a traveler on a journey from trauma to a testimony of God's love and mercy, from struggling with mental health to being spiritually and emotionally healthier.

Friend, I've been so broken only Jesus could fix my messy life, but I'm so thankful for the other tools He provided to help me along the way: His Word; a faithful, godly husband and supportive kids; invested biblical mentors; a skilled therapist; amazing medical experts; a sacred circle of praying sisters; inspiring authors, podcasters, thought leaders, and academic researchers; Bible-teaching churches; and so many more.

Here's the thing: we're all broken. Whether our shattering stems from the actions of sick people with evil intent, our own self-inflicted wounds, or the collateral damage of living in a fallen world where the enemy seeks to destroy, living broken is a jagged edge that cuts everyone deep. I know; I lived like that too long.

This book is for those who know the struggles of trauma—the pain, abuse, and heartbreak—but it's also a story of HOPE. I confess, I'm far from having my life together, but what I've learned running through the valley is it's made sweeter by every stride I take with my Savior.

Throughout this book, we'll often run to Scripture for repeated illustrations of how far God goes to encounter, embrace, and engage the ones He loves by practically encouraging and spiritually empowering the broken, the wounded, and the lost. King David understood this when scribing Psalm 34:18: "The LORD is close to the brokenhearted and saves those who are crushed in spirit."

I know this to be true.

We'll also sprint back into the Bible to demolish demonic lies and, with God's help, answer some of the hardest questions challenging authentic faith.

Along the way, I'll interject ideas and resources from mental health experts and share coping mechanisms that helped me because God continues using them beautifully throughout my journey and beyond.

Paul wrote: "God is our merciful Father and the source of all comfort. He comforts us in all our troubles so that we can comfort others" (2 Corinthians 1:3–4 NLT).

Take comfort if you're troubled. Come walk with me.

When I undertook documenting my trauma therapy journey in the early fall of 2019, I wondered where this whole story would take me. I had doubts about how it would end. Unable to remember most events of my childhood, how could I presume to fix the troubles stemming from it?

What I've found is that in God's perfect timing, with His resources and the Holy Spirit, my limitations and doubts don't matter. What matters is faith, hope, and love. What matters is Jesus, true family and friends who fight and pray for you, who go with you the extra mile and help shoulder the boulders and weights threatening to crush you until you're strong enough to carry them yourself, or, even better, until they are removed.

Friend, you are here for a reason. If somehow you hold this book in your hands, read it on your device, or listen in on my podcast—it's no accident. The story ahead is for you or for someone you love very much. Either way, don't ignore God's message, whatever His message is for you.

Let's walk this journey together.

— Leigh xoxo

She Seems So Normal podcast

PART 1

MY "NORMAL"

Origin Stories Helped Shape the Plastic Princess

As a kid in the '70s and '80s, Saturday mornings sometimes meant window-shopping at the mall with my mom and sister. Whatever was displayed in the window determined my enthusiasm for the store. I was always intrigued by the mannequins. How serenely statuesque and poised they appeared. Adorned and accessorized, they reminded me of Princess Diana, so the lovely mannequins morphed into "plastic princesses" that I imagined myself being one day.

In 2003, after committing my life to Christ, I looked around at women in the church and was not only amazed by but secretly jealous and covetous of their seemingly perfect Christian worlds. I saw examples of the Proverbs 31 woman, submissive wives with a godly lives, Dave Ramsey–enveloped finances, Dobson's well-behaved children, Joanna Gaines–inspired houses, find-my-strength-in-Jesus bodies, and noteworthy religious social behavior. I attempted to internalize the "too blessed to be stressed" bumper stickers and "give it to God" plaques.

For the record, I don't believe there is anything wrong with doing good works, living right before the Lord, or setting a blameless example for others to see. Nothing is wrong with biblical finances and parenting, honoring our bodies, or having hospitable homes. We should strive to do this as Christians. My problem stemmed from allowing the enemy to twist my perspective about my precious sisters to believe in the possibility of their perfection. Or mine.

Only Jesus Christ is perfect.

But through this crooked lens, everywhere I looked, everyone seemed like they had it together. Except me. Setting out to copy everything I observed in the women I respected at church, I attended Bible study, memorized Scripture, stopped cussing, gossiping, and getting drunk, and cleaned up my act. Serving in any ministry that would let me, I did whatever was needed. Heck, I served till the cows came home because I was just so thankful Jesus saved my soul from hell, and I desperately longed to prove I was worthy of His sacrifice.

But putting lipstick on a pig doesn't make it a lady. I was doing all the right things, the things I saw others doing to be good Christian women, but I wasn't trying to heal what was broken and hiding within me. So, I developed a veneer, a mask.

Before I realized it, I became a plastic princess.

Even after many years serving and leading inside church, always with a nebulous undercurrent of shame, I somehow felt like an impostor in my own skin or a mannequin dressed for display. Deep inside was a mess I couldn't identify or fix no matter how I served Jesus or the church. I tried a "factory reset" each time my mess went sideways—behind the scenes, at home, or in my head.

What I know now is that when you scratch the surface of anyone's life, most "normal" people deal with shame, whether it's from past or present sin or faith struggles or mental health issues or whatever. I discovered I preferred covering and hiding mine. The enemy loved it because he loves keeping things in the dark.

What's the peskiest problem of being a plastic princess?

When

The Fire

Comes,

It

All

Melts.

In part 1 we walk together on the journey that exposed the plastic princess I formed and how the Lord began to show me hope. It will sometimes be raw, but it's real, and the only way to move past brokenness is to start there. Part 2 gets meaty and challenging and just plain hard, but it's legit watching God and others help me through the vulnerable, ugly mess. Finally, part 3 showcases key lessons I'm learning that the Lord has illustrated in the valley and punctuated throughout my climb out the other side.

My promise: it ends waaaaay better than I ever expected God could make it for me. So, take a deep breath and smile because "the peace of God, which transcends all understanding, will guard your hearts and your minds in Christ Jesus" (Philippians 4:7).

Note: At times, this journey documents raw sections containing vague descriptions of abuse. While I did my best to be sensitive and not trigger survivors or abusers or traumatize support people, inevitably, some stories within these covers may cause a visceral response. Skim those sections but press into others as God prompts.

She Seems So Normal podcast

Chapter 1

THE HARDEST STORY
I NEVER SHARED

If you have faced abuse or trauma or walked with those who have, you know sugarcoating reality doesn't let light into the darkness. Why are there horrific stories to tell in the first place?

Struggles go back to the beginning in the garden of Eden. Although God gave Adam and Eve abundance and fellowship, they ate the forbidden fruit (Genesis 3). As the serpent hissed with delight, Adam and Eve hid, guilt-ridden and full of shame. They knew they did wrong (eating the fruit of the Tree of Knowledge of Good and Evil), which changed their *identity* (realizing their nakedness).

As you read my story and consider your own, remember the garden. But don't stop with the sin of Adam and Eve. Don't wallow in guilt or shame.

Remember Adam and Eve and the fig leaves? They couldn't hide the shameful private parts peeking through the foliage.

So, what did God do? Though they were guilty, God used animal skins to cover them.

That's what God does—it's what he did for me. By the blood of Jesus, He covered my shame and forgave my guilt. It has been a long journey to learn this truth, one that took me down a dreadful path at the US Military Academy at West Point.

👑 A Hard Question—Why Didn't I Leave the Room?
14

After thirty years, I never understood why. What I know now is I never considered it a viable option. I've rarely shared this story because of my shame. Many think they knew what happened that fateful spring in the Fourth Regiment's barracks. I was blamed for ruining a "good cadet's career" and called names like "slut" and "whore." Infamy followed me, but I'm silent no more.

My West Point experience gave me nightmares until I came to Christ in my thirties. Now I dream of leading, protecting, and helping others to be strong and victorious.

"Why didn't you just leave the room?" my husband, Christopher, asked me one day in exasperation. Married twenty-

> We feel guilt when we do something wrong and shame we when think we are wrong in our nature. Brené Brown states, "There is a profound difference between shame and guilt. I believe that guilt is adaptive and helpful—it's holding something we've done or failed to do up against our values and feeling psychological discomfort. I define shame as the intensely painful feeling or experience of believing that we are flawed and therefore unworthy of love and belonging."[1]

seven years, we've known each other for thirty, since the day he walked into the room to become my basic training squad leader at the US Military Academy at West Point.

A fair question, one often asked by those who want to understand but haven't faced such trauma.

Between watching my mud-encrusted face as I crawled under concertina wire and my struggles memorizing the requisite bugle notes throughout basic training, Christopher has seen me at my worst. He was also the brave soul in the grenade pit the first time I pulled the pin and tossed one over the concrete barrier. After a firing range sergeant altered my gun sites, Christopher came to correct it, knowing something was wrong when the farm girl used to shooting coyotes and old metal car rims for target practice suddenly couldn't hit her mark.

At the time of my congressional appointment from Wyoming in 1989, women had only been allowed in West Point a short time (the first class with females graduated in 1980). I was grateful for the young women who paved the way for the opportunity to serve in military leadership.

In my only year as a cadet, the first female leader of the corps of cadets, First Captain Kristin Baker, was blasted by cadets even while she was making the front page of the *New York Times*. Some upperclassmen said other cadets were more qualified for promotion and wondered who she'd slept with to get the spot. Others didn't like her high voice commanding the corps from the marching plain or speaking in the mess hall. While my post-graduation military intentions to serve my country were blowing up stuff as an ordnance officer and becoming a translator, I admired Cadet Baker and dreamed of leading like she did. It was not to be.

At the end of basic training summer, I was sitting on standard-issue wooden chairs in our company's counseling room, sweat rolling down my back, pooling at the waist-band of my black athletic shorts. It was brutally hot and humid with no air conditioning. Even with the mandatory open door, I was nervous to be in a room alone with any male cadet, but it didn't help knowing I was letting down my favorite squad leader, Cadet Mackenzie (Christopher).

"People don't want me here. I don't fit in. Nobody likes me. I'm going home, sir," I haltingly announced.

Christopher told me I shouldn't quit because if I did, the people who didn't want me there win. He asked if I was a quitter.

"No, sir!" I wanted to believe it. So, I stayed.

Back then, girls had a snowball's chance in a firestorm of succeeding in the fourth-class system at the military academy. Fraternization—every cadet's terror—was being accused of crossing the strict plebe/upper class, superior/inferior social boundary. Observing friendly "frat" daily between male peers and their male command, I concluded my upline leadership seemingly hated or feared me. Cadets acting kindly or even marginally friendly in their interactions with me were threatened with "fratting" and often became my worst haze nightmare. One junior felt terrible about my treatment during basic training but explained that helping me risked his future. The "problem child" pariah, I became an outcast shuffled through multiple squad leaders throughout the school year.

On evenings when I should have been studying, different upperclassmen commanded me to stand at attention for hours in their rooms, wasting precious time. Sometimes, it was chilly standing against wardrobes opposite open windows, my white athletic shirt pulled taut across my chest and tucked into a mandatory "dress-off" into my shorts. Ashamed as they tittered and pointed to my body's natural response to the cold, I was overwhelmingly relieved when allowed to leave.

Saturday mornings before four-hour calculus tests, other team leaders prepped their plebes with equations and "remember this" theory. Not mine. Entering Thayer Hall in tears of frustration, I wondered if higher math would get me kicked out of USMA. It wouldn't. That test came second semester.

 One Night Changed My Future

Fourth-class freshmen male cadets were often funny and flirty, but honestly, females considered them buddies and brothers-in-arms. Cadet dating was weird, doomed to fail. There were a few cute boys, but I wouldn't have wanted anything to hurt my chances of being a respectable leader.

During basic training, one plebe freshman seemed to like me, but his circles were not my circles. We were in different classes, companies, and barracks. Until that fateful week of spring break when all the upperclassmen were allowed to leave and every plebe required to stay, I saw him only a few times.

Without upperclassmen present, spring break dance parties busted into hallways from the basement rooms below the barracks. Acting like silly, "normal," nonmilitary college students laughing and enjoying life without the usual restrictions, we had the most fun we'd had since reporting that first steamy summer day. The plebe from basic training must have spoken to me at one of those parties. He was cute, so I'm sure I smiled, but when the party was over, everyone went back to their rooms to prepare for Taps.

Details of that night get hazy at this point. Cadet rooms had no locks at that time, so when he knocked and entered without permission, he startled my roommate and me already in bed. He asked if I wanted to go somewhere. I anticipated another dance party, so I reassured my roommate I would safely be back soon. I'd never ask her to lie about my whereabouts because in the military, you don't put your roommate in that position, and I truly believed I would be back. The thought never occurred to ask where this cadet was taking me before we left.

After a while, I remember asking him in the hallway, "Are we going to another party?" giddy at the thought of dancing again.

"You'll see."

What happened next still swirls as dream-state surreality. He led me down labyrinths of stairwells and underground tunnels through unfamiliar hallways, so when we arrived at what I now suppose was the Fourth Regiment's barracks, all direction and bearing was lost on me. Confounded that no one patrolled these halls, I kept following.

Entering a room, I immediately knew it couldn't be his. No patrols, no roommate, and messier than any plebe's room, it must have been in an upper-class area. I should have bolted the second he shut the door, except . . . I didn't realize it was an option. He was a football player, a top cadet in our class, and clearly in control.

When he began kissing me, I thought he wanted to make out a little and go dance. Surely, there's no harm in kissing a boy, right? He was cute, desirable, and more importantly, he wasn't in my company.

My mind flashed back to an event earlier in the week: one of my company peers, a huge football player, pinned me against the wall behind his door trying to kiss me. The lights were bright, the hallway noisy. Yelling expletives, I squirmed and shoved, ducking under his massive arms and out of the room. With other cadets in proximity, he easily let me go.

This was different. No one was about, and he didn't turn on the lights. Although my eyes had adjusted to the dimness, I hadn't seen the blanket between the beds. In my confusion, with shirt and clothes thrown suddenly to the floor, he quickly progressed to pushing me down onto the blanket.

Begging him again and again not to do this, I desperately asked him to use a condom. Make no mistake, my begging was not sexual foreplay, and asking for protection is not saying yes. My mind caving to the inevitable was somehow strategizing staying ahead of a potentially more devastating consequence. The terror of pregnancy ending my military career trumped being raped.

He refused.

When he was finished, I lay unmoving on that blanket, paralyzed with shock. How had this happened to me?

Unsure what to do next, I considered leaving but quickly realized I had no idea how to find my room. Fearful of cadet patrols catching me and more fearful of the discipline I'd receive—walking hours in full military dress—what could I do? I stayed.

A loud double knock and a bright flashlight startled me. I gasped. The patrolling security officer strode in, spotlighted me, and quickly backed out of the room. He yelled for us to get dressed.

My regiment's security had found me. In my company, I was unaccounted for at bedtime, so they searched every room, every barracks to find me. The other cadet had covered his bases. No one reported him missing at Taps.

How did I return to my barracks? It's blurry. I only recall showering in my company's latrine, scrubbing my skin to expunge the filthy way I felt and smelled. Lying naked on a towel atop tiny, unyielding, military-approved tiles, I cried myself to sleep.

"We didn't know where you were," my roommate said. "I told them you went with him."

Early that next morning, he knocked brusquely, entering my room again without permission.

"You will not speak of anything that happened last night. Not a word. You won't tell anyone anything. Do you understand me?" His words hit like kill-shot bullets directed at my soul. Standing still as a statue, I gazed out my window at the Washington Monument on campus.

At this point as I write, my brain echoes my trauma therapist's words: "Where are you feeling this in your body?" The honest answer? I feel my heart exploding for all I lost with my next words:

"Yes, sir."

The day I gathered enough courage to explain the night's events to a lieutenant colonel, he shamed then blamed as he informed me that men's hormones run faster than women's. "You should have known to leave," he said. "It was your own fault." According to him, I guess I got what I deserved.

Let me be clear, what I faced there was not acceptable. It never is. But misogyny is hard to break when it's the status quo and you are powerless, whether as a first-year plebe at a military academy or a pioneering female in a male-dominated culture.

My favorite aunt and uncle supported me at the conduct board trial. After grilling me for details of that night, my lawyer uncle swore and said, "Leigh Ellen, you have to say something. Tell what happened to you." My automated, programmed military response: "I am responsible for my actions and the actions of those around me."

"Cadet, do you have anything to say in your defense?" Silence rang in my ears after the tribunal officer's question. Shaking my head, I whispered, "No, sir." Across a barrier, I remember my uncle's and aunt's loving faces becoming downcast with disappointment after the judge's pronouncement. We were both kicked out but allowed to stay until the end of the semester to complete our freshman studies.

Until I mentored other college rape victims years later, I never realized how unjustly I was dismissed from West Point. After confessing this to my uncle, he looked at me with kind, understanding eyes and said, "I know. We've always known."

Redeeming the Shame

"Why didn't she just leave the room? Why wouldn't she report it?"

When I've heard others speak these words, I can't tell you how many times I hid behind my plastic mask, silent, too afraid to betray that I've been "that" girl.

Predatory grooming is a form of learned helplessness and trained powerlessness. It's like a baby elephant that's chained to a stake and repeatedly attempts to escape. While she's little, the chain and stake hold her in place. Once grown, at full size and strength, she could easily pull up the stake to break the shackles, but she has learned helplessness. Isolated, broken, trained, and exploited, she can no longer use her special God-given elephant gifts of beauty and power. Human grooming and intimidation that encourage, overlook, ignore, or enable predatory behavior—like the learned helplessness of the little elephant—perpetuate continuing abuse cycles in places like military academies.

The culture at the military academy solidified an aspect of the plastic princess I became by reinforcing earlier grooming and learned helplessness. Now, when my own beloved West Pointer asks me why I didn't leave the room, I can explain why.

You wanna kill a dangerous snake? Don't play pattycake. Crush its head. That's what Jesus did.

In Genesis 3:15, God said to the serpent, "I will put enmity between you and the woman, and between your offspring and her offspring; *he* shall bruise your *head*, and you shall bruise his heel" (ESV, emphasis added). This has been called the "first gospel" in Scripture because in this verse God shows that although satan will bruise the heel of Jesus at the cross, ultimately Jesus will crush his head.[5]

> Learned helplessness is a state that occurs after a person has experienced a stressful situation repeatedly. They come to believe that they are unable to control or change the situation, so they do not try—even when opportunities for change become available.[2]

Update on the Military Academy

"The women in the Class of 1980—the first to include female cadets—were able to say unequivocally they were treated differently because of their sex. They spoke of the assaults and harassment they faced both at the academy and once they entered the Army.

"Brig. Gen. Cindy Jebb, who now serves as the Dean of the Academic Board at West Point, arrived two years later as a member of the Class of 1982. Looking back at her cadet career she said, 'I think it's safe to say we were probably all sexually harassed.'"[3]

As recently as February 2022, *Washington Post* Pentagon correspondent Karoun Demirjian reported more than 130 documented sexual assault cases (a 48 percent increase from the previous year) at the three US military academies.[4]

I could never get past the shame, blame, and guilt I experienced from others who abused me, but this momma elephant is finally learning her strength and identity in Christ to find her voice. Borrowing courage from women who have spoken up to put entertainment moguls, morning talk show hosts, and millionaire financiers behind bars, I hope to blaze new paths, encouraging others to speak up and stand shoulder to shoulder in these battles.

Verses to Consider

Genesis 3:1–15

Romans 3:21–26

She Seems So Normal podcast

Sexual Assault Support Resources

Use your smartphone camera to scan and go directly to these resources.

Rape Abuse and Incest National Network (RAINN)

If you or someone you know has been affected by sexual violence, RAINN's sexual assault hotline offers free, confidential, 24/7 support in English and Spanish at 1-800-656-HOPE (4673) and online at RAINN.org y en español a RAINN.org/es.

National Center for Victims of Crime

ChildHelp Child Abuse Hotline
1-800-4-A-CHILD (1-800-422-4453)

Victim Connect Resource Center: 1-855-4-VICTIM (1-855-484-2846)

National Teen Dating Abuse Hotline: 1-866-331-9474

Chapter 2

SYSTEMATIC GROOMING NORMALIZES ABUSE

Throughout my childhood, there were several seasons when people who were older than me and in a position of responsibility exploited their authority, thereby grooming me. If you aren't familiar with the term in this context, here's the working definition.

Grooming defined: According to the National Society for the Prevention of Cruelty to Children (NSPCC), groomers build relationships, trust, and emotional connections with children or young people for the purpose of manipulation, exploitation, and abuse. Groomers can be any age, gender, or race and may also "build a relationship with the young person's family or friends to make them seem trustworthy or authoritative." Grooming can happen over weeks or years.[1]

What follows are just a few personal stories at various ages illustrating how predatory abusers systematically program environments around their targets. In the final portion, I also detail some of the lasting, residual effects of my grooming.

♕ Episode 1 (Junior High): The Everyday Monster
4

Sometimes "everyday monsters" aren't the wealthy, rich, and well traveled; they're the people who build your schools and hospitals, coach your kids, or work in the cubicle next to you. These are the everyday things that can happen to everyday people by everyday monsters.

By the age of three, my parents were divorced, and my dad was absent from my childhood. As I searched my world for kindly father figures, I was desperate to have someone in authority who seemed to really understand my struggles, fears, and hurts to give me the esteem and confidence I lacked. In middle school I thought I found that person in my coach.

Pulling into the parking lot, music blaring over the Jeep's speakers, hair wild from the wind blowing as he drove without the doors and top on, he quickly came to a stop and began pulling bats and balls out of the back. Every girl on the team loved him because he encouraged us, laughed loud, and often made jokes at practice. Even when we lost a game, he wasn't like other coaches who yelled; he had this positive, can-do attitude that was infectious, especially for discouraged girls with low self-esteem like me. Always smiling, he seemed like the adult who just "got" a bunch of crazy, hormonal girls. In our little town at the base of the Rocky Mountains, he also owned a sub shop serving the best banana shakes on Highway 86.

One day, he asked if I needed a ride after practice, and I said yes, though the tavern where I walked to meet my mom after practice was only half a mile away from the ball field. I'm sure to Emerging-Teen Me, being singled out felt great, even for such a short drive in a cool Jeep with Coach. This became the regular thing, these drives and the talks about life, boys, and softball.

The summer before my sister left for college, my mom went through a big breakup with the guy we'd lived with since my parents divorced. Everything familiar dissolved. My mom and I searched for a new place and a new way to live. Though I don't clearly recall every detail, Coach came to the rescue, offering me a chance for summer employment at the sub shop. This job seemed to relieve my mom of caring for the immediate issues of what to do with her tween on the long summer days, plus it put cash in my pocket. Coach, now Boss, taught me privileged information—how to make my favorite shakes, open the register, and keep secrets.

At first, after a few inappropriate, off-color jokes, we laughed heartily, and he begged me not to get him in trouble by telling my mom. At age twelve or thirteen, I had tons of private thoughts I'd never blab to her, so his silly sex jokes barely registered on my radar. Preoccupied with body odor, makeup, music, my weirdly blossoming body, and how to get boys to like me, I shared my deepest and darkest concerns with him. He always laughed and sometimes had good advice, I'm sure. After all, wasn't he a grown-up, a man full of wise answers and encouragement?

Though I don't remember every conversation's details, I know I trusted him deeply and believed he really cared for me as a coach and a boss. I yearned for a father type to cherish me, even by throwing a ball around, and he seemed happy paying attention to my needs.

Sometime toward the end of the summer, he began dating my mother. Weird because, well, he was my coach, then boss, now friend. He came over a lot. While he charmed my mother with his words, he sat on the couch and tickled me. Tickle fights slowly turned into wrestling matches, most days right in front of my mom. Bored, she'd leave.

Maybe my mom attributed this horseplay to my tomboy personality and his playful, seemingly fatherly relationship with me. Rolling around on the carpet laughing and sometimes panicking when "play fights" ended with me pinned helplessly beneath him, what had started out as fun began to seem more like power struggles that he always won. After a while, he'd let me go and we would laugh it off, like it was my misunderstanding.

At some point, he presented a set of extravagant gifts: a double-cassette eighties boom box, three cassettes (Olivia Newton-John, The Police, and Men at Work), and a set of Mikimoto pearls with matching earrings.

In the dog days of August, just before school started, someone decided the three of us should head north on a little trip to stay in a grand hotel at a beautiful national park. Together.

It was in the enormous white-tiled bathroom that I began bleeding. I probably shrieked, completely embarrassed knowing that Coach was there, sitting on the bed in the other room. Thinking I was dying, I sobbed louder. My mother came in to ask what was wrong. I think I told her, "I have cancer," and she laughed and said something like, "Silly girl, you just got your period." I had no idea about what it meant to begin menstruating; she never mentioned this would happen—it was probably a generational thing. Apparently, I didn't listen during fifth-grade sex ed. Still to this day, I have no idea why I was so shocked and unprepared, but considering it now,

I wonder if the gift of womanhood before seventh grade came in the nick of time to save me from something awful happening in the hotel room that weekend.

Unfortunately, it didn't save me that night in the tropics or later at West Point.

Episode 2 (Age Thirteen): A Grooming Story with Lowballs, Ice, and Vesco

A memory I've always had, forgotten, and remembered again at random times—the narration changed as a fuller picture emerged.

Vacationing in Central America for spring break, I was now a teenager, around thirteen years old. A well-dressed older man was visiting with my "grown-ups" over drinks in the hotel bar. The nightlife scene was loud and raucous as voices and music echoed off floor tiles. The fans circling lazily overhead looked overworked and about as tired as I felt after a long day in the tropical sun.

Distracting myself with people-watching, I imagined stories for each character who entered and left the bar lounge. Sometimes, people would notice me, a young, blonde, and blue-eyed girl in a very grown-up, dark-hair-and-eyes environment, staring at them, so I'd smile and quickly look away, embarrassed about getting caught spying. Occasionally, as shouts and laughter of one group markedly rose to a crescendo above the rest, a door would open, and I could hear the staccato of scattering cockroaches on outdoor patio tiles as they raced to get out of the light. Though it was the best hotel in the city at the time, nothing kept out the cockroaches in the tropics—be they insect or human. Nothing.

Ice clinked against lowball glasses as grown-ups discussed Noriega's Panama, how lawyers and financiers are the real power in any country, and a man named

Vesco. The well-dressed man bragged about being one of Robert Vesco's lawyers, something which seemed to impress my grown-ups immensely.

For me, it was blah, blah, blah. I was a bored teen, but I remember parts of this night clearly for some reason, especially the ice and Vesco. In Central America, ice was a big deal to me because it melted so fast my soda was never cold. Apparently, Vesco and anyone associated with him was a big deal too.[2]

While I don't recall why I left with the fancy lawyer or what was said, I do remember standing up and smoothing the wrinkles out of my outfit, hoping I didn't have any embarrassing sweat stains. Suddenly, three of us were walking through sketchy streets in the dark. (His bodyguard had silently joined us.) As we sauntered through the neighborhoods, the man talked about the power dynamics of countries, how the men to be feared weren't the ones with military weapons but the ones who had men carrying guns inside their jackets. He motioned to his associate who nodded, patting the black metal bulge inside his blazer. Throughout the winding walk, my safety assured because of the hidden firearm and these men protecting me, I thought, *Why am I here? Who is this man giving me a history lesson?*

Walking into a building down the hallway into a less-than-pristine room decorated with seventies goldenrod-yellow decor, the bodyguard stationed himself outside while the man opened the door for me. I heard electricity buzzing in the room's lighting. The man undressed, sat on a wooden desk chair, its cushion covered in a golden damask print, and whispered quietly, calmly, seductively to me.

In my mind, I've always told myself that I boldly spoke up that night, telling him I'm not that kind of girl, and he allowed me to leave. The reality? A man powerful enough to have a bodyguard outside a hotel room door would never let a girl leave until he was finished with her.

The rest of the night always hazes into a blur. The only thing I remember is walking back with his bodyguard to my hotel. Without him leading me to a sidewalk running along the freshly tarred parkway to the Mercado Central and hotel lobby, I could have never found my way back.

I cannot remember anything else about the rest of the trip. Eventually, when memories flooded my mind in May 2020, I realized I was probably trafficked to the man, and though I never received a single coin for all he did to me in that dingy yellow hotel room, I will now never forget its horrors.

Check that—God in His great kindness and mercy continues to help me forget.

> Let those who love the LORD hate evil,
>   for he guards the lives of his faithful ones
>   and delivers them from the hand of the wicked.
> (Psalm 97:10)

Praise God for delivering me from wickedness—I made it out alive. And my story can offer hope to others. Keep reading. You'll see.

Episode 3 (Adult but Triggered Back to Toddler): Grooming Story Affecting My View of Men with Special Needs

The encounters I had with men, whether a coach over a lengthy time, a one-time event on a short trip to Central

America, or others not mentioned here, shaped not only my perspective of myself but of others. This led to unfortunate conclusions I unwittingly drew about some groups of people. For instance, events in my childhood affected my view toward men with special needs for a long time.

Men with special needs terrified me for most of my life. I never understood why my heart raced or why I wanted to run except that they seemed unpredictable. I worried they could hurt me somehow, even though logically I knew they wouldn't.

A few years ago, right in the middle of some kid's birthday party, the Lord helped my mind release the answer at the weirdest place: an old bowling alley. You know the ones that have musty, cigarette smoke–stained carpet, loud jukeboxes, and the best french fries?

A local Special Olympics team was bowling that day, and the men boisterously cheered and celebrated. Observing from a distance, fear struck my heart; instinctively, I moved behind my husband for protection. A distinct memory fluttered to mind, one I could never reconcile until then.

Three or four years old, in a place with many rooms flowing from one to the next, I was at a wild party. Making my way through a sea of legs, loud, drunk men kept trying to pick me up to hold me. A squirmy toddler not wanting to be held close, especially not to rough faces or masculine smells, I kept thinking when they caught me, *You are not my daddy. Stop touching me*, and I pushed and fought so much they couldn't hold me at all. I remember the feeling of falling, being dropped multiple times.

What I also understand now is that is one of the first steps of the grooming process for a child to be sexually abused—getting used to being touched or held close in front of other adults. The strong, slurred speech of loud, drunk men from the past triggered my fear of the loud men with special needs at the bowling alley.

How like the serpent to deceive and create terror of the innocent and kindhearted. He distorted my reality by turning these men into monsters in my mind. Once I understood the memory and response, I didn't have to be afraid of our sweet friends anymore.

Train up a child in the way he should go;
even when he is old he will not depart from it.

—Proverbs 22:6 (ESV)

Childhood grooming is the antithesis of the Spirit-breathed meaning of this verse. One of satan's greatest ploys is twisting what God intended for good and using it for evil.

Five Things to Know About Grooming

1. *Groomers aren't always who or where you might expect.* They can be spouses, high-level leaders, or workout buddies or people inside your family, community, workplace, or church.

2. *Predatory abusers choose their targets and environments carefully.* My friend's wife was a clinical narcissist who groomed and controlled him to feel like a total failure. Onstage he was a powerful teaching pastor, but within the walls of his own home, he was terrified and terrorized by her.

3. *They groom the room.* Masterful at normalizing questionable behavior, groomers train target environments for months, even years. (Consider toxic corporate, institutional, or national environments of systematic racism, religious intolerance, misogyny, and bullying. Or consider most people of color in America, former Playboy Bunnies, child TV stars, or Olympic gymnasts.)

4. *Trust your gut and ask the difficult questions.* Parents, teachers, mandated reporters, responsible adults, or peers: if something's sketchy, seek wisdom, resources, and help.[3]

5. *Honoring children's personal boundaries hones their instincts.* Allowing a child to say no to unwanted touches—even innocent ones—and honoring those requests gives the child permission to trust his or her own interpersonal radar.

Verses to Consider

Psalm 97:10
Proverbs 22:6

She Seems So Normal podcast

For more information on grooming, visit the National Society for the Prevention of Cruelty to Children.

Chapter 3

TESTING GOD,
TOUGH QUESTIONS

*The damage done through abuse is awful and heinous,
but minor compared to the dynamics that distort the
victim's relationship with God and rob her of the joy
of loving and being loved by others.*

—Dan B. Allender, *The Wounded Heart*[1]

It would be so easy to play the "I hate God" card when bad things happen to us or to people we love. It's difficult to understand God's goodness and His greatness while we live on planet Earth. If He is good, why is there evil, and if He is great, why doesn't He do something to help a sister out? Why do we, as Christian believers, go through unpleasant or horrific times? Why do we have to suffer?

We can certainly ask, "God, where were you when this happened?"[2] That's honest. God is big enough to handle a question like this from us. If we're lucky, He may even answer in our prayer time, in visions or dreams, or through godly people and circumstances in a way that never contradicts the whole and complete counsel of Scripture. Or He may not.

Can I be angry with God? Can He handle that, or do I need to keep these feelings on the down-low? Will He discard me for any hint of disobedience or disbelief? Is He bigger and better than that?

After all, He *is* God, right? Can He handle a mere mortal honestly doubting or questioning? Can He forgive this rebellion too?

He can and He will. He did it for the nation of Judah in the Old Testament; how much more is he willing to receive a Spirit-filled, gentile Christian like me?

Can I Be Angry with God? (12.10.2019)[3]

[5]

Each morning, listening to my Bible reading plan while getting ready allows me to multitask and meditate while moving forward with my day. One day while washing my face, my ears pricked up at Jeremiah 33:3.

"What was that?" I asked aloud. Hands slathered in thick winter moisturizer, I hurriedly smeared cream on my cheeks, forehead, and neck, rubbing the rest on my arms so I could pinky-tap pause and scroll down on my phone.

The heading read "Promise of Restoration": "This is what the LORD says, he who made the earth, the LORD who formed it and established it—the LORD is his name: 'Call to me and I will answer you and tell you great and unsearchable things you do not know'" (vv. 2–3). The Scripture details how God would allow the Babylonians to tear Judah apart because of its wickedness, but He reassuringly added:

> Nevertheless, I will bring health and healing. . . . I will heal my people and will let them enjoy abundant peace and security. I will bring Judah and

Israel back from captivity and will rebuild them.
. . . I will cleanse them of the sin they have com-
mitted against me and will forgive all their sins of
rebellion against me. Then this city will bring me
renown, joy, praise and honor before all nations on
earth that hear of all the good things I do for it; and
they will be in awe and tremble at the abundant
prosperity and peace I provide. (Jeremiah 33:6–9)

Fears of the unknown have played hide-and-seek with
me throughout this journey of memories, those repressed
involuntarily, forgotten completely, or suppressed intentionally. As I called on the Lord, I anticipated that He
would teach me many great and unsearchable things in
that season. Knowing that "desolate waste" feeling (v. 10),
I trusted the Holy Spirit guiding me in health and healing,
rebuilding the life that God originally intended for me and
ending my rebellion against Him with joy and gladness.

Rebellion? Yes, R-E-B-E-L-L-I-O-N. Rebellion. I
never thought that's what it was, but it's true. Resisting
God's authority over parts of my life, I refused to trust
that He was truly good (loving, kind, forgiving, merciful,
grace-filled) and truly great (all-powerful, all-knowing,
ever-present).

Maybe I'm the only one, but have you ever wondered:
If God is good, why would He let terrible things happen to me?
and *If God is great, why couldn't He stop them from happening?*

Am I a heretic for thinking this of the Creator of
the universe, my King and Savior? I should have just
been thankful Jesus died on the cross without questioning the past.

However, inside of the context of my intimate,
personal relationship with the Godhead, this would be

dishonest, a cover-up. I'd either be making excuses for God (which, let's be serious, is just plain ridiculous and means He is not good or great) or not wholeheartedly believing in who He is, His character, and His intentions toward me. By withholding my deepest, most fearful concerns, I doubted God completely by not asking Him the hard questions directly.

Holding an enormous pink fairytale lens over any indications of frustration or anger when I've read certain Scripture, I've almost "Disneyfied" the big emotions of those holding the pens to the parchment, quipping "all's well that ends well" while ignoring the possibility that those real-life human scribes, empowered with the breath of the Spirit, embodied genuine pain or forthright fears and wrote about them, just like I do.

18

Enter Moses. What follows is my "Disneyfication" of the prophet-lawgiver:

Patiently inerrant, epically holy, the shiny faced, bearded old man stands barefoot etching rock tablets as fire flashes exclamation point ideas from God. As if he's some secretary scripting details of holiness and asking God, "Should we lay off that next cup of coffee? It's been forty days now, sir."

Sometimes I forget Moses was a real flesh-and-blood dude with real flesh-and-blood problems interacting with the One who created the universe and called us into existence. I've applied the rosy lens instead. Biblical people didn't have plastic, but I've read about many who put on religious facades like we do today, but not the prophets or psalm writers.

The Psalms and the books of the prophets are rife with raw emotion, revealing sincere, vulnerable questions along with outrage, soul-cries of kings and seers calling on heavenly mercy.

After accurately recognizing the Lord's indignation at Israel's collective sin, Moses readily confessed in Psalm 90 while proclaiming his distress in the oldest recorded psalm, "Relent, LORD! How long will it be? Have compassion on your servants!" (v. 13), fervently challenging God while acknowledging His divine anger. The "friend of God" expectantly awaited abatement of national affliction in answer to his pleas. But, man, when you read in Exodus how many times those mutinous Israelites longed to lynch Moses, you'll understand why the man slow of speech and tongue quickly shouted his real feelings to the God of all power and authority. Sadly, the prophet's anger tripped him up at the end, when, instead of speaking directly to God about it, he unleashed it on a rock for all to see. The punishment? Moses never stepped into the earthly Promised Land.

A man after God's own heart, King David penned Psalm 23's comfort amid trials, resting by still waters through shadowy valleys of death, not fearing enemies or evil, to remind us of Emmanuel—God *with* us. However, what about Psalm 13:1 when David cried out in anger, "How long, LORD? Will you forget me forever? How long will you hide your face from me?" and "Look on me and answer, LORD my God!" (v. 3). But the shepherd-king always came back to praise by the end of his rants:

> But I trust in your unfailing love;
>   my heart rejoices in your salvation.
> I will sing the LORD's praise,
>   for he has been good to me. (vv. 5–6)

David's psalms teach that you can be angry with God, but you shouldn't stay there too long: always end in praise and thanksgiving.

Moses, King David, I feel ya here. Thanks for showing me I can have momentary anger yet still trust God in the end.

Burned Hands and Baklava

16

It always goes back to baklava these days.

"New year, new you." For my daughter Bella and me, 2020 meant trying new adventurous recipes. We decided to make baklava on our own at home for the first time.

My friend's Lebanese baklava recipe was complicated and contained unfamiliar ingredients and techniques. Six cups of finely chopped walnuts are copacetic, but three and a half sticks of clarified butter, phyllo dough, and a lemon simple syrup weren't in my cooking arsenal. Clarifying butter was not something I had done, but the recipe called for it, and my twelve-year-old talked me through removing milk solids from oil to make ghee. I wanted to try my hand at it.

Bad idea.

Long story short: don't melt butter in vintage Pyrex liquid measuring cups over open flames. Long story long: with a burned hand and butter still in my hair and on my clothes, I wrote with one hand, documenting this mess.

How did this all happen?

The cracked Pyrex was a simple, amateur mistake. The butter was melting nicely over the flame on my stove when I heard a strange noise. As I reached for my favorite four-cup measure, I saw the glass cracking internally with a lightning seam from side to side.

Bella inquired what happened, and I exclaimed that the heat had split the glass. Wasn't Pyrex heat-tempered, for heaven's sake? "No," Bella told me, eyes rolling. "You should have done it in the microwave." (Methinks I got schooled in cooking by my tween over Christmas break.)

After pouring the butter into another container to cool and separate, I examined the five-inch crack. Was this measuring cup still usable? Sadly, I knew the answer was no. To the trash my favorite and most useful piece of Pyrex went.

Rest in peace, dear Pyrex. Rest in peace.

Walking into the kitchen, I smiled at the sight of Bella dipping a sandwich into ketchup and relishing the taste. I addressed the clarified butter, now separated, by stirring it slightly. My hand brushed the still-hot sandwich press Bella used to make her grilled cheese. My finger was only slightly burned, but I cried out, surprised at being hurt by something I didn't realize was dangerous.

Upset at Bella for not warning me that the press was hot, I sternly told her that the next time she used it, she needed to keep it open so it would cool faster and to warn people it might be hot. When I asked her about it later, she told me I didn't yell. At least therapy's helping.

With massive emotions brewing below the surface, I walked to the bathroom to cry. Strange? Yup. I wasn't really injured, more surprised than anything, but for inexplicable reasons, panic overwhelmed me. The hyperventilating began.

Praise God, I communicated clearly between sobs. I responded to Bella's apologies, telling her it wasn't her fault but I was having a panic attack. Her arms around me felt like a saving angel's hug. I began alternate nostril breathing to calm myself, and three to five minutes later, my emotions receded as I gathered my wits. The entire episode lasted ten minutes.

Sitting at my computer later trying to comprehend what had just happened, I thought, *What prompted this illogical and unnatural response?* After reading the paragraphs I had written, the answer was clear: I was hurt out of the blue by something I hadn't realized was dangerous or could hurt me.

This revelation helps explain my life. At critical times, people trusted to care for and protect me did not, and others I trusted one minute couldn't be trusted the next. Unpredictable environments and people are the hallmarks of alcoholic, abusive, or dysfunctional families. "Little Leigh" had little stability with things being fine one second but not the next.

Here's my pattern:

Calm > Pain > Surprise >Anger > Panic

This recurring pattern usually happens with people I love the most. Life's fine and dandy until pain surprises and catches me off guard. A teenager's cutting, smart-aleck remark after asking him to clean up for the nth time cues me flying off the handle. My husband's cold fingers touching warm bare skin get slapped with surprise, fear, and discomfort. Hitting car breaks while I'm your passenger prompts audible gasps and a frightful clawing of legs.

But whatever you do, don't jump scare or grab me. We'll both regret it.

♛ Anger Flare

¹⁷
A friend around church loves to jump scare his wife and other people. Thinking it would be funny to sneak up unnoticed, grab my arms, and yell "Whaaah" when I was otherwise engaged was his big mistake.

The moment his hands touched my shoulders, my military training and survival response were automatically triggered. Squatting, I threw up my elbows and hammered him before thinking twice. He was on the ground for ten minutes, and while I tried to comfort him in his pain, my heart felt awful, but my mind vacillated between being angry he surprised me and feeling upset I lashed out violently. The "anger flare" had happened within seconds as my panic and pain flashed, shooting from zero to ninety, out of control.

And, now let's resume our normal broadcast . . .

When I physically injured myself on the sandwich press, the pattern began, and I was immediately enraged by pain striking intimate, personal, hurt nerves from oh so long ago. Anger flares usually end in various panicked reactions: regrettable words, embarrassing actions, and occasionally, hyperventilation.

That's so dumb, isn't it? Yet, it's the reality in which I've often lived. Know anyone like me?

> No natural feelings are high or low, holy or unholy, in themselves. They are all holy when God's hand is on the rein. They all go bad when they set up on their own and make themselves into false gods.[4]
>
> —C. S. Lewis, *The Great Divorce*

Anger flares, I realize, are from the inner child not being allowed to safely express big emotions. Stuffing down anger and unforgiveness over years creates emotional bombs biding their time, waiting for the right spark to detonate. Can you imagine the explosion damage from people so emotionally dry, spiritually raw, physically hurting, and completely unsupported? Boiling to the surface unchecked and unmanaged, violent anger flares are destroying families, schools, and workplaces and dividing cultures, communities, and cities across America.

Another thing about the pain of childhood trauma: my brain doesn't distinguish between intentional or accidental pain or physical or emotional pain but instinctively responds viscerally instead of analytically filtering it with logic. That's gotta change, because if it doesn't, I remain a hostage inside my own body's memories. The only answer is forgiving and releasing these ancient hurts through God's Word, the Holy Spirit, and professional trauma therapy.

Solomon sprinkled the book of Proverbs with countless golden nuggets to establish successful planning strategies, including how to wage war and win. What's his advice? Gather good and godly guides. Check it out:

> Plans fail for lack of counsel,
>> but with many advisers they succeed.
>
> (Proverbs 15:22)

> For lack of guidance a nation falls,
>> but victory is won through many advisers.
>
> (Proverbs 11:14)

> Plans are established by seeking advice;
> so if you wage war, obtain guidance.
>
> (Proverbs 20:18)

Since my plan is victory and this is spiritual warfare, I'm definitely gonna need good and godly advice.

Friends, here's the personal inventory at this point: (a) God is for me and only gives good gifts to His children. Even when I'm torqued, I can safely run to the Father knowing He won't give me stones or snakes. And (b) I am going to need a lot more people to help me with this journey.

Verses to Consider

Proverbs 26:11
Jeremiah 33:3–10
Matthew 7:9–11

She Seems So Normal podcast

Chapter 4

ON THE LOOKOUT FOR WISE COUNSEL

My memory during those early days of therapy was like a wisp of smoke.

Today, I see it as one of the most powerful ways God has showed His love to me.

Since beginning therapy, memories have kept crashing into my everyday life. Suddenly, as I smell something or see images flashing through my mind, anxiety rises, my brain chemicals bubble, and with those images come the memory: the time, place, and person. I think: *How had I forgotten to remember this one?*

Then, as soon as I remember, I forget. It's almost like looking into a box I packed long ago and immediately thrusting the lid back on it. This is how I have always dealt with memories: fearfully, self-protectively stuffing them into boxes and shelving them. This time, however, I'm pulling a Marie Kondo (the Japanese organizing genius) by detailing and chronicling every item, as if documenting and categorizing it for later analysis.

Wait. I am categorizing for analysis.

Writing each event and committing it to paper or pixels reestablishes timelines. Identifying and understanding memories that have lain dormant for decades provide foundations for triggers I'm experiencing in the present.

How did I never notice them or that I was being triggered so much? Why do I react in a certain way when I feel certain feelings or emotions?

In Proverbs, Solomon wrote,

> When wisdom enters your heart,
> And knowledge is pleasant to your soul,
> Discretion will preserve you;
> Understanding will keep you,
> To deliver you from the way of evil,
> From the man who speaks perverse things.
>
> (Proverbs 2:10–12 NKJV)

Truly, God has offered me wisdom with these life-long trauma-plagued behaviors and habits. With safety on all fronts and under the care of amazing professionals, family, and friends, the season for deep and profound healing is upon me. Finally relinquishing all territory, I have handed over my deed because He's not just my Savior but the Lord over all.

Master, my lands are yours, all the chickens, bees, and apple trees, my soul proclaims. *The gifts, talents, sin, history—it's all yours. My exhausted soul lays bare for your examination,* with the desperate afterthought, *Just heal and take it all now.*

Have I finally come to the end of myself? Will I truly trust and become honest with God?

I won't get there without some serious deconstruction and restoration along the way.

👑 Deconstructions Begins: Plastic-Princess
9 **Deconstruction Moment #1**

Paul seemed to be able to rise above people-pleasing better than most of us. He wrote, "Am I now trying to win the approval of human beings, or of God? Or am I trying to please people? If I were still trying to please people, I would not be a servant of Christ" (Galatians 1:10).

Bully for him because it's not as easy for me. Desperately wanting to please and serve well, I have spent my life trying to make people like or approve of me. On the surface, this is not bad, but a highly desirable trait of competent employees. However, when the desire isn't balanced, the trouble begins.

Longing for love and healing and finding it in all the wrong places, when I got disappointed in the past, I felt used. Not receiving gratification, affirmation, and acceptance from the outside made me miserable on the inside. Wrapping my identity up in other people's approval is part of being codependent—I recognize this now.[1] How often did my joyful satisfaction originate with the Holy Spirit? Good question.

This I knew: I needed help to sort out my life. And God sent me the perfect helper.

👑 How I Met the Doctor
8
I met Dr. Michele Novotni in the summer of 2019. During a Christian conference in Grand Rapids, she kept trying to talk to me from the first roundtable meeting, and I could not understand why. Dr. Novotni was an established professional author many important people

seemed to know. Why would she spend any time with a nobody like me?

The first night, she said she'd save me a seat at dinner. I didn't go. From across the room the next morning, she motioned me to sit by her at lunch, but the table placements went awry. Finally connecting the last night, we exited the conference center together, exhausted from a long day of sessions.

Dallying as giant parking lot lights buzzed above us, we chatted about wanting to use our God-given spiritual gifts for kingdom work when I noticed a strangely familiar, hand-woven, silver-interlaced, and three-dimensional necklace.

"Your necklace is Guatemalan, right?" I asked.

"Yes . . . ?" Michele answered with a thick Philly accent I loved, her smiling brown eyes looking deep into mine.

"Was it made in Antigua?" I questioned because I'd been outside the same tall, whitewashed wall surrounding the silver factory there as a teenager back in the eighties. My mother had a similar necklace in her jewelry collection.

"Yes. It wasn't finished, but since it was the one I really wanted, I waited until the artisan was done and actually bought two of them. I paid full price and didn't even barter," she said. "I made the lady selling it smile. That's what matters, making people smile," she said, tilting her head at me knowingly.

From this friendly, love-fest moment forward, that silver necklace confirmed God sent this brilliant woman to be my sage, seer, and guide. What I didn't know was how much I would rely on her wisdom, vision, and expertise for my own healing and freedom in the coming months.

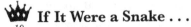

If It Were a Snake . . .

19

How many times have I missed people God sent or refused help? While God may have sent a variety of messengers for me, I was too blind and deaf before now.

"If it were a snake, it would have bitten you!" is my usual Colorado farm-girl response. "I mean, it was right in front of you," I say to myself and usually out loud. "How could you miss it?"

When Michele and I met in Michigan, she was retired, living in Florida, and I lived atop a bluff city overlooking the Mississippi River. With absolutely no way we would have ever met, it had to be God's plan, right?

An experienced psychologist, Michele knew the end game—once I faced my demons, things would improve. If I discovered the problem's root with careful cognitive examination and professional analysis, my beliefs would change.

Funny, I almost missed this mentor, except she kept after me. God clearly had sent her, yet I kept (unintentionally?) avoiding the woman. That, or I was being kept from her.

Countless times, her encouragement kept me from quitting, but as you will read, many have walked on this long journey with me.

Full disclosure: it's rarely a solo gig following Christ. Alongside Michele, my boss and longtime friend Allison, and my therapist, I cultivated a rotating powerhouse of "battle buddies" back in 2018 assembled from women all over the world.

A posse of prayer warriors and cheerleaders encouraged me and expected me to keep moving forward in battle. These battle buddies kicked me in the butt, equipped me for spiritual warfare, and encouraged me to do anything I was avoiding. I wanted to give up when I felt too far gone to be "fixed," but these accountability partners checked in weekly after appointments, verbally processed emotions with me, and kept cheering. Reassured of straight-fire prayer support when the enemy attacked in the middle of the night gave me peace in daily battles. Quitting halfway was not an option, and summoning strength to begin again later was too much to consider. For heaven's sake, we were never promised later—we only have today. God held my hand through the most despicable, horrifying parts of my past while my posse fought in the heavenlies in the present. Without help, I had no way of escaping the enemy's slimy torture pit or my own melting plastic facade.

Here's a funny story how Michele brought joy to the journey through my valley.

 Red Christmas Trees
20

"Absolute perfection belongs not to man, nor to angels, but to God alone."[2] John Wesley wrote this, but my inner perfectionist tried to prove him wrong. One Christmas, as we opened gifts in front of the fire and our fire-red Christmas tree, we were enjoying a peaceful and quiet morning. Sipping creamy coffee in holiday jammies, I contentedly watched our kids open carefully curated presents.

As the gift opening wrapped up, I gazed out the window, enveloped in a peppermint-daydreamy, blissful state until . . .

POW!

Shocked and startled into cold reality, my eyes wide and my heart racing, I shrieked. Bella, the little stinker, had popped air-filled plastic packing bubbles with scissors. The sound was louder than thunder to me.

Suddenly, my eyes filling with tears, I began to cry uncontrollably—as in frightened baby-type crying—unable to stop or understand what in the world was happening. Why was I crying? I was just scared, but that's not a normal adult response to kids popping bags. My fear turned to embarrassment, which then morphed into shame.

With genuine concern and confusion, both my teen and my tween exchanged wide-eyed, shifty, nervous looks. *What upset Mom?*

After I told them I was all right and had no idea why I reacted this way, Bella told me, "Mom, it seems like your emotions are really near the surface these days."

She was right.

When you're doing the difficult work hashing up the past, digging deep to kill scary monsters in the closet, it's emotional. Surface tension waits for the next demanding memory, PTSD flashback, or unexplained knee-jerk response to kick your butt.

Feeling like a failure, these two flash point incidents magnified how I wasn't managing life and responding in the ways "normal" people respond. This realization immensely motivated me with deep indignation to remain unwavering and steadfastly under the therapy umbrella. Because of these flash points firing more often than ever, I was seriously thankful for expert coaching.

As I took my dog for a walk, I called Michele to explain what happened with the burned hand incident I mentioned in chapter 3. She was thrilled, happy to hear how well I was doing when I finally successfully employed the strategies we had developed over the past few weeks.

"What?" I asked. "Are you kidding me? I feel like a complete failure. These attacks keep happening, Michele. What's wrong with me?"

"Oh, no!" she said. "Look how far you've come. You've been using the tools in your toolbox to help you get through these attacks. Before you wouldn't have been able to handle them as well, would you? That last attack only lasted about ten minutes? That's great. I'm so proud of you for not yelling or getting angry with Bella. And you put into effect the breathing techniques I told you about in addition to adding yet another tool that is helping you analyze what happened." She continued in a sing-song voice, "You're writing about it. I'd say you've had a win-win-win-win here."

"Then why do I feel like such a loser?" I asked. "These keep happening, and I am not handling them like I should."

"You've been pushing down pain for forty-something years," Michele responded, "and you've only been working through it all for the past month or so. Did you expect to be perfect at managing these so soon?"

"Well, I expected to be better than this . . . yes."

"Leigh," Michele said, "that would be like you deciding a month ago you were going to run a marathon and now four weeks later, thinking you were ready for Boston."

"Ha-ha, yes. You're right. It must be a little of that perfectionist in me coming out, huh?"

"Ya think?"

I wish everyone in the world had someone like Michele in their corner. Actually, it might be beneficial for us each to look around since I'm betting God's providing a mentor right now for you too. Remember: you don't have to walk this journey alone.

Verses to Consider

Psalm 1
Proverbs 11:14
Proverbs 12:15
Proverbs 19:20
Ecclesiastes 4:12
John 1:5
2 Corinthians 10:4–5
Galatians 1:10
James 1:5

She Seems So Normal podcast

Chapter 5

THE CHILDREN AT WAR
WITHIN ME

As an internal recruiting consultant to a Fortune 300 company twenty-five years ago, I supported hiring efforts for an incredible distribution business unit manager responsible for more than five hundred employees. Can you imagine the issues and problems such a high-level leader deals with from day to day?

Once, I asked her how she kept everyone on task and on mission. She smiled, looking across the desk, and told me, "Sometimes people are easy and fun, but when they're complaining, aggressive, or acting like babies, I wish I had a giant pacifier to shut them up."

Yeah, me too. Except the people I wanted to shut up were inside my head.

Little Me and the Living Room of My Mind

21

Do you ever wonder why normally rational, calm people suddenly act childish after conflict or even seemingly mundane events? Why do they regress to junior high behavior or worse, acting out and throwing grown-up temper tantrums? It's almost like some inner child emerges and takes over for this seemingly grown human being, sometimes in shocking ways.

Over my life, as a result of the many traumas I've suffered, many "children" from every stage have screamed inside me. As I've encountered situations that reminded my brain or body of former times of stress, abandonment, or abuse, these children have been triggered and acted out behaviors that worked in the past. I have noticed their traits more and more as I have uncovered my timeline memories.

Here's an example:

My husband and I normally have breakfast, lunch, and dinner together. We co-parent our children, living, working, and doing ministry side by side. I'm blessed that during the most intense portions of therapy, he rarely left town for work.

One day, Christopher announced at lunch that he was going to have a fairly busy travel schedule throughout the upcoming month of May. As a thoughtful husband, he considerately gave me a heads-up so I could have time to plan kid and work schedules.

It shouldn't have been that big of a deal, but in a split second, panic arrived. May, as every mother with school-aged children knows, is insanity. It's the end of the school year. Music concerts, school parties, awards ceremonies—*everything* happens at the end of the school year. I hadn't even considered teacher gifts at that point.

I was triggered: I felt massively abandoned. How could Christopher leave me at a time like that when I needed his help the most? This feeling turned into frustration as I considered everything that was happening on top of my regular duties at work in addition to those as the grocery getter, taxi driver, dinner maker, cleaning lady, and dog mom. Then I grew angry and felt betrayed beyond belief. In my downward spiral, a pseudo-funny thought crossed my mind: *Should I ask for the divorce now or when he gets back from the trip?*

Seriously, I'd lost it.

What was this all about? Why was I, a fully capable parent and adult, internally freaking out and feeling this way?

As I have been learning throughout this healing process, it all goes back to the childhood memory markers imprinted in my brain. The feeling in the present with my husband drew me back to a day that my father had left me, perhaps traveling for work or maybe for the final time. These links between past and present are why trained professionals play key parts reconciling this journey.

My dad's Karmann Ghia convertible was parked on the street that day, and I distinctly remember grabbing his leg and begging him not to leave while my mother pulled me away screaming. I can still see his little red car driving down Lee Street, suitcases filling the passenger's seat, and feeling abandoned and oh so alone without my daddy.

The panic and insecurity of my husband traveling, of parenting our kids alone deepened the desperation of three-year-old Little Me wanting her dad. With my need for security feeling ignored after my father left, the present trigger of my favorite man in the world leaving for business unleashed a watershed explosion of primal emotions from forty-plus years ago.

The grown-up part of me knew I could handle anything that came my way. I had a proven track record as a capable mother, but Little Me suddenly popping into my conscious mind, crying *We've got no one to help us, we're all alone, and how can we handle it if something terrible happens*, became my undoing. What was the source of her hijacking power?

As a child, Little Me needed protection from everyday predators, someone who recognized the abuse signals when a normally compliant child exploded into legendary temper tantrums when pushed too hard to comply. Did no one see or act? What is certain is no one rescued. I suffered decades from things that happened during the first half decade of my life.

In light of these revelations, with help of my therapist and friends, I have been paying attention by rescuing and comforting Little Me in her fears. After all, I am an adult. And adults don't freak out in front of children. So that day, I said to my little self, *We hold so many tools and resources. We can l handle anything while Daddy's gone*, and it was true. I had way more resource support than scared Little Me was given.

I imagined myself as Little Me in a house I created in my mind. Grown-Up Me was sitting in the living room on a green mid-century couch. Tears overflowed from her wide blue eyes, her little button nose reddened from wiping snot with the back of her hand. Patting the cushion, I motioned for her to come sit closer. She ran, hopping a little. I lifted her from under her arms and into my lap. We faced each other, and, with a meaningful look, I smiled and brushed soft wisps of hair off her round baby face.

Little Me sobbed. "I'm scared! Daddy's going away again and remember what happened last time?"

"I do," Grown-Up me said. "But this daddy is not that daddy. He is a totally different person; he's not your daddy. He is your husband."

"Don't daddies leave you forever?" Little Me asked. "And don't others hurt you because they're gone? Who's going to protect me from bad men that come?"

"I am going to take care of protecting and caring for your needs, Sweetie. No one is going to hurt you again like that. God is watching over us and will send His angels to protect us."

"How?"

"We pray," Grown-Up Me said. "And I'm really good at protectively caring for people. Don't you remember my military year? I would fight till death to save you from harm."

"Really?" Little Me asked.

"Trust me, Sissy. I got this."

"What if you don't?"

"Then Jesus has us covered."

These are the types of conversations I have now in my head as I re-parent the single-digit girl who still lives inside me in terror. Slowly, we are learning to work together. I'm learning to validate Little Me's feelings and affirm her reactions while she learns Grown-Up Me will never abandon her and will protect her from danger of any kind.

Does this sound crazy? I hope not, but there are so many times I was traumatized in some way, and these reactions come up whenever the situation seems the same. Instead of responding as the grown-up that I am, I react like the hurt child, triggered particularly when the classic HALT circumstances often taught in recovery circles hit me: Hungry, Angry, Lonely, and Tired. I like to also include a P for Painful, so HALT becomes PHALT. Through this process, I've identified three stages of me: Little Me (three to five years old); Middle

Me (six to twelve years old); and Teen Me (thirteen to eighteen years old).

If we are not trained with positive coping tools during childhood or disciplined through loving support as big or overwhelming emotions arise, we can act like children well into adulthood. After five decades walking the earth using behaviors that ceased to successfully work long ago, I have been learning to make different choices, developing healthier, more spiritually sound behaviors that serve others at the same time.

So, when I hear Little Me rising to the surface, I search and identify the specific feeling I am having by asking myself, *What's this big emotion? When and where have I felt this before, and why?* In so doing, I identify each Little Me directly to internally re-parent her with what she needs to feel at ease once again.

After talking to Little Me that day, she became calm for the moment, wrapped contentedly in my arms on the green couch. However, another me, who's equipped with more sophisticated resources and toxic reactions, lurked and scowled through a dark doorway at this sweet scene. Her name? Teen Me.

What to Do About Teen Me?

Have you ever seen an angry child who's never been appropriately calmed, lovingly disciplined, or given boundaries? That little person will grow to be a big person with that angry child still inside. Anger and hurt will simmer just below the surface and explode under turbulent conditions.

Around age twelve or thirteen, hormones added to the crazy cocktail stirring inside of me—the passive child became a really angry teen. My internal methods of coping with childhood trauma began breaking out externally and often. Over the course of a decade, my emotional and psychological conflict continued to brew as my brain mulled complicated questions. *Am I unlovable?*

Honestly, I wanted to take a knife to those around me, but guilt and shame made me turn the metaphorical knife on myself because I was simply incapable of deciding what else to do.

With life so out of control, I took the reins the only way I could: I stopped eating. When I was so hungry I couldn't help myself, I would binge, eating everything in sight, vomit, then feel satisfied I was able to control *just one thing.* Since all I wanted was to disappear, this was the way my teenage mind arranged to do it. We'll call this girl "Teen Me."

My outside appearance seemed normal. A typical tween-teen, my focus throughout junior high was divided among grades, sports, and boys. A straight-A student on top of teams for volleyball and basketball, I was attracted to all the wrong boys. How wrong? Two of them ended up in state prison. Yeah, take that in.

At that point,

1. I didn't believe I was worthy of anyone better, and
2. I believed I deserved everything I got.

These twin lies were the ultimate weapons of sabotage coming straight from the enemy. This hatefulness spewing from the pit of hell I agreed with and affirmed regularly, its daily repetitive onslaught taking its toll on my thoughts, emotions, and attitudes. Feeling unworthy of real love, I acted upon it by doing wretched, unholy things. As a teen, I didn't know how to take my thoughts captive and be obedient to Jesus because I didn't know my Savior then.

Books tell you that the milestones and concerns for the tween-teen stage typically center on the struggle for identity. *Who am I? How do I operate socially? What kind of person do I want to be? Who do I identify with?* Students in this age group look for good and bad role models and imitate behaviors, trying words and actions on for size. Ask any parent of a tween or teen, and they'll tell you this age group stretches boundaries as they spread their wings and begin to determine what their growing independence from their nuclear family looks like.

What I am learning is my Teen Me was blindly furious, completely uncontrolled, verbally caustic, dangerously treacherous, and ridiculously manipulative. She was a teenager, right? This girl was downright scary because she had no idea who she really was and no safe identity model to follow. Threatening personal injury, suicide, or binge drinking when she was mad or after she disappointed others, this one fantasized about literally disappearing and running away from home. She exploded like a time bomb—3, 2, 1, 0. KABOOM!

At this point, I have yet to confront Teen Me. Honestly, she scares Grown-Up Me a little, but I have a feeling I've already worked with her for years during my time as a high school small-group leader, and what I know is this: almost every teen girl is desperate to be fully and unconditionally loved.

As a teenager, I wish I had known that God loved me absolutely and delighted in me, that I was fearfully and wonderfully made in the His image for a holy ministry on earth and a glorious eternity in heaven. These revelations didn't come for another twenty years or more.

Standing in the doorway of the living room of my mind that day Christopher told me he would be traveling, I watched Teen Me with her arms crossed, shaking her head. She flipped me the bird, muttered something incoherent under her breath, and retreated into a back room, slamming the door.

In Mark 3, even after a shriveled-hand Sabbath healing in the synagogue, epic disease-healing events, and exorcising demons from the masses, Jesus's family called him crazy, and teachers of the law claimed His power was in concert with Beelzebub, the prince of demons. Jesus responded: "If a house is divided against itself, that house cannot stand" (Mark 3:25).

Throughout his earthly ministry, empowered by God, Jesus helped people clean house emotionally, spiritually, and corporately. He restored the blind, lame, and leprous, offered demoniacs seasonal spruce-ups for sound minds, and parabolized finding lost coins, recovered lost sheep, and brought sons back under the same roof (Luke 15). Christ's death, resurrection, and glorification bind us as heavenly family, adopted as sons and daughters through His sacrifice; they unify us in one mind, one body, one church.

At the moment, I'm wanting this to happen in my own body. In the meantime, Little Me hums constantly, playing with her naked Barbies on the carpet, as Middle Me silently engrosses herself in a stack of books. As they play on the battleground of my mind, my expectation is the battlefield will rapidly shrink the healthier I get, thereby allowing Jesus to be Savior AND Lord over all the territories of my life.

If you take nothing else away from this book, I pray you read these next words:

Regardless of everything you've done or that's been done to you, the Father has never, ever let go of you or left you. He's seen it all and is not disgusted with you or ashamed of you. God wants every line of promised Scripture to give healing and freedom. He brings darkness to light, so take every thought captive in obedience to Christ, demolish strongholds, and utilize the lavishly gifted divine weapons of the Holy Spirit to move forward in faith.

Verses to Consider

Proverbs 1:1–8
Proverbs 3:5–6 (OK, just read all of Proverbs!)
Mark 3
John 1:1–5
2 Corinthians 10:3–5

She Seems So Normal podcast

Chapter 6

11

IS MENTAL HEALTH THE NEW LEPROSY IN CHURCH?

Through December 2019, an Instagram sister walked alongside me, and over Christmas, her entire family was upended by an abuse revelation. I prayed fervently, standing shoulder to shoulder with her as she sought help and counseling. I video called her weekly to chat and pray over coffee; she told me that my being open about my trauma therapy on social media gave her the go-ahead to seek counseling for herself. Over time, others have also written to thank my online pen-name persona "The Church Girl Writes" for my transparency and honesty about mental wellness and getting help for anxiety and depression—especially since I worked inside the church.

Many well-meaning Christians will tell you to "cast your anxiety upon Jesus because He cares for you." And He does. Sometimes, they quote clever soundbites— "You have to give it to God" or "You're too blessed to be stressed" or "Don't worry, pray!"—or offer other pseudo-helpful platitudes. Quoting Scripture *at* someone is not the same as praying *with* or *for* them. Why are people afraid to come alongside messy? Could we contract it?

I wonder if mental illness struggles represent the new leprosy inside the bride of Christ?

No one wants to talk about it or touch it, and if you say you're getting counseling, people appear nervous or seemingly avoid you each time you enter the room.

What's the issue when it comes to social-emotional-psychological maladies? Surely, we could overcome our brains' wiring by the Holy Spirit alone without seeking medical advice? But why should we create such a high barrier when the Lord provides doctors, counselors, therapists, and medicines to help? You'd never tell a person with hypertension or angina or diabetes or thyroid problems not to seek medical help or take their medicines. Never.

Hear my heart, I'm not saying people are wrong or that Scripture isn't true; it's just that there's a little bit more for those who suffer from panic attacks, clinical anxiety, ADHD, or depression or for those suffering from trauma, abuse, or neglect.

An article at Care Net makes this point:

> Just like with a physical illness, often the Church doesn't have the medical expertise to heal the person struggling with mental health. So, just as with physical illness, the one struggling should seek professional medical help. God can heal any illness; however, he can use whatever means he chooses to bring help and healing through support of medical professionals, family, friends, or the Church.[1]

God has given us medical doctors for treating illnesses when the physical body breaks down. He has also provided mental health professionals for treating the emotional and mental breakdowns we face.

Here are some statistics from Lifeway Christian Research from 2018:

- 23 percent of pastors acknowledge they have personally struggled with a mental illness.

- 49 percent of pastors say they rarely or never speak to their congregation about mental illness.

- 27 percent of churches have a plan to assist families affected by mental illness.

- 65 percent of churchgoing family members of those with mental illness want their church to talk openly about mental illness.

- 59 percent of those actually suffering from mental illness say the same.

- 53 percent of churchgoers with mental illness say the church has been supportive. . . .

- 68 percent of Americans feel they would be welcome in church if they were mentally ill.[2]

Do you find these stats astounding? They are from 2018, well before the pandemic launched a world trauma outbreak physically, emotionally, and socially.

Condemnation Is Neither a Spiritual Gift nor a Fruit of the Spirit

In times of deep depression before therapy, there were seasons I needed medicine to keep myself from considering permanent solutions to temporary problems. Wanna know what was scarier than considering suicide? Believing I was unfit and disqualified—not just for Christian service within the church, but as a Christian.

Speaking to my boss and dear friend one day who was also a leader in our church, I told her she needed to fire me, or I was going to quit.

"You can't have a crazy person serving at the highest levels inside a church," I pleaded. "I have never known the kind of constant, regular peace with Jesus like I have using the medication I'm on. I doubt my salvation because maybe the Holy Spirit never took hold (even after I was baptized and my faith confirmed miraculous change). There's something wrong with me, Allison. Why in fifteen years haven't I ever had normalized amounts of the fruit of the Spirit, love, joy, peace, patience, kindness, goodness, faithfulness, gentleness, and self-control? What's wrong with me?"

Encouraging me out of crippling self-condemnation and despair, Allison told me it was sin not to take the medicine my doctor prescribed. She gently reminded me that through the many years she had known me, the works and fruit of the Holy Spirit were obvious and evident and said that I shouldn't doubt my salvation.

Now that she knows my entire story, I imagine she is amazed I'm functional and appear so normal, given my background and the crazy stress hormones bathing my brain since birth. The hypersensitivity and attention to detail, the people-pleasing and situation-controlling persona that make me a powerful addition to a leadership team were all birthed in the abuse battles I survived as a child. For that, I suppose I am thankful.

What Is Courage?

There was a season I marched through eye movement desensitization and reprocessing (EMDR) therapy and boldly braved whatever came my way, but I only did it without medicine because I had to feel emotions and pay attention to cues my body gave. Not everyone needs to do that. Convinced this deep healing season was appointed by God, I laid down my need to numb, avoid, or dissociate from reality to get to the truth of what happened long ago.

According to the EMDR Institute, eye movement desensitization and reprocessing (EMDR) "is a psychotherapy that enables patients to heal from the symptoms and emotional distress that are the result of disturbing life experiences." It is "recognized as an effective form of treatment for trauma . . . by organizations such as the American Psychiatric Association, the World Health Organization and the Department of Defense."[3]

Others remarked at my courage, but I didn't feel courageous, only terrified, afraid of really knowing and afraid of never knowing. If courage equals the ability to persevere and withstand danger, fear, or difficulty, any courage people see in me is because of the Holy Spirit, and I keep clinging to the cross and the resurrection of Jesus Christ. Knowing God has the power to raise men from the dead, I know He can raise me too. After He raises my dry and dusty bones up out of the grave and breathes life into them, He can surely use me to encourage a vast army of others to do it too (Ezekiel 37:1–14).

Is it no wonder that there is fleeting peace for trauma survivors? How can we find peace in the middle of a

PTSD event?[4] Abuse victims with flashbacks and triggers are like soldiers coming back from nightmare scenes of battle—we may be intact, but we are emotionally, mentally, physically, and spiritually damaged. You cannot unsee what you've seen or undo what's been done. You learn to live again and find ways to cope.

God has given me many coping gifts. Turning my consciousness away from what happened to my body, He has given me the "gifts" of dissociation, amnesia, and the ability to simply forget people's faces. I'm thankful to remember few faces of the men who abused me.

The Lord gave fierceness and elasticity to me as a young child. Even the most delicate glass doesn't always shatter when dropped, but I was dropped many times. Refusing to break completely and bouncing back again and again, I fought my way back from the depths.

Full disclosure, that bouncing wasn't without collateral damage. Taking responsibility for my poor choices in reaction to my circumstances, I repented, turned away from those sins, and did my best to reconcile with those I'd hurt to repair the mess. Continuing in the process of sanctification (being made in the likeness of Christ), I am hopefully growing in divine grace the longer I walk with Jesus.

Michele once told me shocking statistics from the organization Darkness to Light (www.d2l.org) that pedophiles and child molesters can destroy the lives of up to 40 victims over a lifetime. I don't doubt the figures. My abusers loom in my mind as monsters from the past, gigantic dragons the Lord and I are vanquishing one by one. God willing, my story might help you or someone you love to move forward to seek help and find freedom. I pray for just one more person to find an intimate personal relationship with Jesus to encounter saving grace and mercy. God can handle your messy. The Father loves you right where you are, and if you follow the Son, He'll take you where you need to be so that in Holy Spirit power you can be more than a conqueror.

Unholy and Made for Destruction

31

I first sought EMDR trauma therapy in 2019. It was late in the fall, a time of year when the leaves constantly change colors—green to gold/scarlet/tangerine to brown—fall, and then die. Looking at the trees outside the window, I contemplated how my relationship with Christopher would change if I healed. Could our entire marriage dynamic shift after twenty-five years of playing the same roles? Could we survive? With God's help, we could only get better. Here's why.

During one extremely low point almost a decade earlier, the enemy convinced me (using Scripture, no less, from Romans 9:16–25) I was an unholy vessel fit for destruction. He argued my faith wasn't real, that my regeneration and new life were lies. Sound like the "father of lies" was doing his thing? Yep.

He reasoned: "Why do you keep going back to your sin like a dog to its vomit? Why can't you stop sinning? It's because you don't have the Holy Spirit; your confession was a lie. You didn't 100 percent believe at baptism, did you? You doubted. You're. Not. Saved. It's an abomination you teach Bible study and act like you know God's Word yet not live like you should. Ask your children, your husband . . . the people closest to you know the truth. You are unholy, meant for destruction."

Any of this sound familiar to you? I hope it doesn't, but if it does, you need to hear something: you're not alone.

Suffering in silence behind fake smiles at church, work, or school, feeling like impostors, we believe if people knew the real us, shockwave tsunamis of relational repulsion might rip everything apart. Is any sin too great for God to forgive? And even if He does forgive, will other Christians turn away in abhorrence?

I know. I've been there, swallowing those lies hook, line, and sinker. The enemy ate me for lunch and spit out my bones.

One sunny day when my kids were twelve and seven, there was typical kids' chaos going on in my house. After all, it was summer and between the chaos of dirty floors, rooms, and laundry, buzzing flies getting in from unclosed patio doors, and the noise of kids being kids, I blew a gasket.

Instead of acting like a parent, I erupted, triggered by the chaos. Middle Me and Teen Me and I veered out of control with anger. Screaming at my kids, I ranted so much, the yelling strained my vocal cords.

My ears rang.

My head hurt.

My voice cracked.

At one of my lowest parenting points, the enemy began whispering again, "See, you can't control your temper. These poor children, see how you damage them? You're a terrible mother. What if we played a video rerun at church Sunday for everyone to see? You. Aren't. Saved."

Sobbing in sorrow, it seemed he was right.

Then d'Evil[5] began convincing me to carve the word *UNHOLY* into my arms and across my chest with a butcher knife so that churchgoers could read what a fraud I was. Thankfully, I was too paralyzed to make it to the kitchen.

My greatest shame is reporting both our children witnessed this entire attack with their mother moaning incoherently on the stairs. In distress, my son called Christopher to come home at once from work.

On my knees, I remember begging Christopher to end our marriage misery, commit me to whatever insane asylum would take me, and throw away the key. I pleaded with him for divorce so he could find a more suitable wife and mother for our kids.

He refused.

I don't know why.

"We will find our way through it somehow," he said. Always, he has been the one fighting for me to live, fighting for our marriage even as it hung by tattered threads.

Birthed from a year suffering from insomnia, frustrations with parenting, and feeling overwhelmed by what felt like impossibly hopeless circumstances, this embarrassing episode, I now know, contains marked panic attack responses. Unfortunately for my family, at that time I had negligible coping mechanisms and would never ask for support with something so shameful as wanting to carve words into my flesh lest other church people confirm my worst fears: the possibility I truly was unsaved and unfit to serve.

How many times are we tempted to agree with the enemy instead of God, to believe we are unholy, though the blood of Jesus fills in the deepest wounds satan could ever try to inflict?

Within weeks, while ending a conference session on suffering I taught in 2015 to more than five hundred women, I referenced this episode as a creative, descriptive euphemism from stage because it held such powerful imagery. Not a single person listening to the message—not the audience, the people in the tech booth or the greenroom, or those online—had any idea this occurred as an actual, real spiritual battle. Except Christopher.

34

Praying fervently as we embarked upon the trauma therapy saga, the Holy Spirit specifically prompted Michele to share with me that Christopher had to be on board in the prayer department. "He has to be EARNESTLY praying for you. Capital E, capital A, capital R . . . all caps EARNESTLY! Do you understand?" she reported emphatically by phone. Neither of us had any idea what that meant or how that was different from "regular" praying, but only that it was really important.

Christopher prayed, I knew, but what did it mean for him to pray earnestly?

While we sipped wine on the couch together after work, I mentioned this conversation to Christopher, even spelling out EARNESTLY for him, like Michele said. Neither of us understood how his prayers would affect and protect the ministry ahead or how his throne room requests and petitions would sustain our marriage and increase our love for each other in the coming months and years.

Now that I can look back, I implore you: stand amazed at the power of a righteous man's earnest prayers for his troubled, sick, and sinful wife! I couldn't have made it without him.

> *Is anyone among you in trouble? Let them pray. Is anyone happy? Let them sing songs of praise. Is anyone among you sick? Let them call the elders of the church to pray over them and anoint them with oil in the name of the Lord. And the prayer offered in faith will make the sick person well; the Lord will raise them up.*

If they have sinned, they will be forgiven. Therefore confess your sins to each other and pray for each other so that you may be healed. The prayer of a righteous person is powerful and effective.

—James 5:13–16

Verses to Consider

Joshua 1:9	2 Corinthians 7:9–11
Ezekiel 37:1–14	Galatians 5:22–23
Acts 4:5–14	Colossians 3:11–12
Romans 8:1–2, 37	1 Peter 5:6–8
Romans 9:16–23	

She Seems So Normal podcast

Lifeway Christian Research

What is EMDR?

PTSD defined

Reflections from Part 1

Shame stories we have created for ourselves cut deep.

1. Shame stories surrounding mental health are a huge issue. Shame stories about mental health struggles as a Christian? Well, those narratives are boss level.

2. Shame stories are narrated by none other than d'Evil.

We try our best to have the mind of Christ, but even as Christians, we must live in the biochemistry our bodies are given. How can we help but feel like a failure unless someone else speaks up to reverse-groom current church culture? I guess I'm going first.

PART 2

UNPACKING "NORMAL"

God Provides a Way Through Every Valley

One morning in the fall of 2019, before 2020's world pandemic even blipped on radars, I was dreaming, plainly hearing the words from Psalm 23:4. "Even though I walk through the valley of the shadow of death, I will fear no evil, for you are with me; your rod and your staff, they comfort me" (NIV84).

What a way to wake up in the morning. Who wouldn't want to hear whispers of the Holy Spirit speaking God's Word as she sleeps?

A cloud of white, one-thousand-thread count cotton, the duvet filled with down conformed to my body like a cocoon as I entered the twilight state between unconscious and awake. Tucked into a fetal position, I could feel the warmth of my little teacup poodle beside me. Scout spasmodically moved his furry paws, low-growling in his own doggie dreams, chasing squirrels and fiercely barking at other dogs. Subconsciously, protectively, I reached down to comfort him . . . or was it me who needed reassurance?

The air conditioner hummed, pushing frigid air from the source unit through shafts to finally spew into my room. The house was kept cold enough even in the summer for me to be fully wrapped and surrounded with covers, as if I needed a protective hiding place while I slept.

The valley of the shadow of death. . . . What's that about? I wondered. *Why does this seem significant?*

And then I got this spiritual nudge: *Go for a run. Two miles.*

What?

That summer when my daughter's cross-country coach needed someone to help him sweep the slowest runners, I helped, but that season was finished. I was done running. This forty-eight-year-old mom, former military, and college rugby player no longer runs for fun or fitness.

Go for a run.

OK, OK. I knew this feeling, the one pressing me in on all sides by the Holy Spirit, and there was no point in resisting. Popping out of bed, I dressed, and, lacing my shoes at the door, I noticed the plate-glass windows framing a glorious morning.

Yeah, my self-talk cheerleading began. *I'm so glad to be up early and going outside! This will be good.* I set my watch to track mileage and distance. Two miles I could manage, so I was glad this godly instruction seemed like a short and sweet one.

And it was sweet, until I began running. You know, the older I get, the longer my body requires to settle into any exercise. Creaking and cracking as my joints warmed, I regulated my breathing, matching my arm-leg swing patterns. Only then do runs ever feel good.

"Lord, where should I run this morning?" I asked the Spirit to direct me, and I was prompted to turn north on Thirtieth Street and then to take a right on Maine Street.

Of course, I got to run up "High School Hill," one of the longest and steepest in our city. I was doing fine as I crested, out of breath, but still in the thick of it.

Glancing at my watch progressively ticking 0.6, 0.7, 0.8 miles, without nudges for turning or deviation, I continued in the direction I was ordered—straight east. My mind echoed earlier dream words: *The valley of the shadow of death*, signaling me to run exactly 1.0 mile, turn, then retrace my steps home.

As I did, I was astounded. With a cemetery above and one below, I had run right through the middle of them.

Below, the small Veterans Administration military cemetery, the Quincy National Cemetery, gleamed proud as a postage stamp, its precisely groomed greens outlined by the black metal fence surrounding them. Stark-white, identical grave markers were almost smiling, perfectly aligned in measured rows and columns. Death, order, and beauty all at once honored the slain.

The other cemetery grimaced. Various cracked gravestones were spread sporadically in precariously leaning clusters up and over the hill; many had fallen and broken in spotty, dirt-patched grass, the weeds peeking through downed tree limbs. In stark contrast to its counterpart below, left with no apparent order, regular care, or attention, this cemetery looked like a long-forgotten burial ground—a picture of deathly disorder.

Death above and death below, I found my run had taken me through this valley of shadow as a snapshot of what was to come. As I unearthed scattered, dishonored, and decades-abandoned skeletons from the past, could I order them with the respect, care, and love they deserved?

This was advance warning of all God would walk

me through in upcoming months and years. After thirty mind- and Spirit-blowing months, I caught the tiniest inkling of the Father's greatness and His goodness. His omnipotence, omnipresence, and omniscience steadily glimmered brighter the more I trusted and followed, becoming crystal clear from this moment on that my King had planned every detail ahead through this deeply profound, multilayered cake of healing. It would entail entering shadows of the past to witness the enemy's deathly, destructive power wreaked on generations of my family. At times I would beg to die rather than have to feel the painful, tormenting sting of the truth. However, what I knew beyond a shadow of doubt was that Jesus would walk with me through this dismal desert wasteland, comforting and correcting me as we went. He would never, ever leave me or forsake me (Deuteronomy 31:6), but what's more impactful is . . .

He.

Never.

Had.

Jesus had always been there, even in the destruction and what felt like utter desolation, only I didn't perceive it before then.

Soon and very soon, though it would feel like ages before I finished this manuscript in spring 2022, I would know that the Lord was always my shepherd, giving me the greenest pastures of rest and leading me beside still waters. He would restore my soul.

Through this story, we will traverse harrowing valleys, unearthing bones to revisit the darkest memories of ghosts housed in forgotten psychological boxes that a child once used to deny their existence. Unholy voices will howl, cracking and warped like old cassette tapes, attempting to maintain control to underscore their powerful soundtrack to my life. To banish these demons hiding in plain view that endlessly plagued me, we will examine childhood experiences with Holy Spirit–infused fire, wisdom, and truth, seeing d'Evil for the thieving deceiver he is. Light will shine bright in the darkness and the darkness will not overcome it (John 1:5).

I had read Psalm 23:4 before, but during that run, I concluded that verse would be the verse carrying me during that healing season. Michele, my psychologist friend and mentor, recently reminded me of this psalm-inspired run so I could scribe it, recounting details. She also reminded me that this all happened long before I had any idea I would be in therapy throughout the upcoming winter months and beyond uncovering what I will unfold in later chapters. My two-mile run demonstrated the Lord laying solid groundwork for me to trust Him, building the necessary biblical scaffolding that would eventually lift me to breathtaking mountaintop views of His merciful grace but not before protecting my descent and reemergence from the tortuous, brimstone depths of hell.

Who gets the opportunity to know the ending to their journey before it begins? I guess, right now, I do.

She Seems So Normal podcast

Chapter 7

BAKLAVA DAY AND BOXED-UP MEMORIES

Experiencing and Processing PTSD

My first EMDR trauma therapy sessions started in December 2019. Over the next two-plus years, while I unearthed repressed memories buried in my brain and body with my therapist, God never left my side crossing the valley wasteland. With every step of this saga, in addition to my therapist, Michele made herself available to help me process my sessions. Whenever I needed prayer or biblical wisdom, Allison responded. And always—always—my beloved Christopher was there praying earnestly as the battle raged, lovingly holding me through each horrifying new revelation. Your journey may not look just like mine (and that's OK!), but I hope your takeaway is how important trained mental health professionals, godly believers, and, if you are blessed with them, supportive family and friends are to your healing journey. That said, Jesus is the most important person in this story, the foundation and cornerstone of every victory we herald here on earth and in heaven.

The First PTSD Event—The Red Room (12.21.2019)

6   As I poured my coffee that morning, two distinct images flashed through my mind, stopping me dead in my tracks—they were both vivid and repulsive. On large glass-shard canvases, they hang suspended in the expansive black universe of my mental gallery. That must be where so many of my lost memories are kept—in the infinite dark.

Image One: Stubble. An old man's fleshy chin. Capillaries broken; the skin was hued bluish purple.

Image Two: A single hand, the skin was stretched tightly around thick fingers. No trace of bone structure as the hand and knuckles were swollen and reddened, rough, and deoxygenated. There was also some human smell I could not describe that made me nauseated.

I knew this chin. I knew the hand. In second grade, I first met the babysitter's husband.

I realized (and remembered) his breathing problems, the least exertion stopping him, oxygen unable to reach his extremities. A raspy breath, the gravelly voice . . . I began writing, remembering glass shard–imprinted images from long ago.

During recall, interpreting my confounding physical and mental responses became complicated:

- Emotionally and psychologically, I was immediately transported through time and space, becoming a helpless girl trained to compliance by abusers, knowing that my no was always ignored.

- Physically, my heart pounded, echoing inside every cell of my body being viscerally drawn places simultaneously disgusting and stimulating.

- Rationally, my mind shouted, *No! These memories cannot hurt me anymore.*

- Spiritually groaning, my soul cried, "God, help me! Save me!"

How could these images make me respond forty years later? Two simple mind-pictures had the power to derail me, making me feel like a child again. How curious, I observed, is the body's response to memory. Your Red Room PTSD might look different. The body keeps score forever even when our minds forget.

Often referenced by experts, *The Body Keeps the Score: Brain, Mind, and Body in the Healing of Trauma* by Bessel van der Kolk contains a pioneering research approach to trauma healing. Though my brain had attempted to eradicate memories of abuse, this book helped my brain trust my body in explaining my experiences.

After I finished writing the previous paragraphs, I thought I was OK. Christopher was at the gym, offering me some quiet time that Saturday morning, but time and space slipped away as I wrote.

Bing! My phone alerted me I was already late leaving for a lesson in the finer points of a family friend's famous baklava recipe. Do you recall that disastrous day back in chapter 3 when Bella and I made baklava by ourselves? I broke my Pyrex, made a buttery mess, and burned my hand. The event I'm describing now happened earlier, on the day we originally learned to make the baklava.

This story is another critical step in the trauma healing process, though equally painful in its own way.

Dressing in haste, my heart raced. Surprised the time somehow slipped away again and I was now behind schedule, when my husband entered the bedroom, I quickly began verbally processing the two images.

In simply giving voice to their description, more memories washed ashore.

My present-day bedroom dissolved as I found myself traveling back to another time and place. The time was when I was five years old; the place I'll call the "Red Room." Standing in the doorway is a menacing man with purely evil intentions, another man with big hands and a nauseating odor, a man I knew but wished I'd never met. Bathed in reddish light, the room is filled with restaurant tables and black chairs stacked against wood-paneled walls, but no one else was there; I could only see his shadow looming, utterly terrified watching him advance.

Many times, when I'm triggered, my mind transports me to this frightening place at age five. Symbolizing the lowest and darkest of my trauma valleys, the Red Room flashback of absolute terror colors the rest of my life in its sickly hue.

Your Red Room might look different, perhaps as endlessly cycling patients in hospital COVID wards, ICUs, or emergency rooms; marching armed and on-edge through steamy jungles; or standing shocked on the sidewalk after another street shooting. Even if you haven't been the object of abuse or violence, witnessing tragic suffering or loss as bystander, family, friend, or first responder, like soldiers returning from battle, we share similar filter-coloring pain with one another in recalling trauma.

Now I understand more about PTSD flashbacks, but that morning, it felt like it was happening in real time.

As I fumbled for my necklace, my hands were shaking uncontrollably. Sobbing, I groped for the cross, my nonverbal safety cue, and told myself that memories cannot hurt me anymore.

"I am close to the cross and Jesus is with me." Repeating this mantra again and again, my breathing quickened to hyperventilating levels. Lightheaded and dizzy, my lips and nose became numb. I felt Christopher's arms gingerly wrap around me, holding me up, and just knowing he was there to protect me de-escalated the attack.

"These memories cannot hurt me, right?" I pleaded for confirmation.

"That's right, Baby. They can't hurt you anymore," he said.

I'm going to be OK.

I have help.

I have resources.

I have a team.

I have a plan.

I have Jesus.

I am exhausted.

I have to go make baklava.

👑 Baklava Day Analysis (12.23.2019)
23

Thankfully, that Saturday morning went from a complete PTSD-type panic attack at 8:45 a.m. to happily chatting about the holidays and finer points of baklava making with sweet friends by 9:10. Moving throughout the weekend, I boxed any big or negative emotions, stuffing and sealing them indefinitely for later.

By Monday, I looked and felt like a freight train had hit. After processing the incident, terrified of the power my memories held, I began fearing an impending attack could happen anytime. As you might imagine, more than a few questions popped up into my head.

- What the crap *was* that?
- Am I crazier than I thought?
- Why was that memory so vivid and real?
- Can I trust it? Is it manufactured?
- Why did I leave reality?
- What if it happens again when I'm alone or in public?
- What can I do to stop it?

Maybe you can imagine how exhausting just thinking can be for someone with anxiety and perplexing questions like these swirling around in their head. Is it any wonder your anxious friends are so distracted or don't have a lot of energy? It's all going to brain power!

Fortunately, I was able to get counsel from Michele as she traveled before the holidays. I texted her details of the most powerful panic attack of my life, and she responded while waiting for a flight: "Oh, yay! I'm so happy for you! You're moving through this healing process so quickly!"

"Are you *crazy*? You knew this would happen? Do I have PTSD? Stop laughing!"

Michele laughing made me laugh too. Her knowing giggle disarmed me in the best way, helping me realize everything was going to be OK.

"Yes! You've boxed up all these memories for so long. It's like a giant pimple popping. The first squeeze hurts the worst, but from there, you're just squeezing out the pus," she matter-of-factly stated. (For the record, she had used this analogy before. It grossed me out then too.)

But it made sense.

Giant pimples feel so much better after you relieve the pressure, don't they? Like pimples, memories and emotions have festered, buried below the surface. In the past they emerged as mismanaged behaviors timed inappropriately, like blowing up over something innocuous with the kids, my husband, or with extended family and friends.

This gargantuan pimple had emerged right on time. However, with all due respect to my friend Michele, I prefer describing it as going in and out of a valley.

While walking this healing journey, I've realized my mastery of boxing and shelving highly emotional or traumatic issues indefinitely in massive mental vaults. Someone with "normal" patterns can actually use this in very healthy, mature ways, shelving big, immediate issues for later processing.

But birthed feet first and breech in a third world hospital, I entered this broken world with a bang punctuated by my mother's pain and doctors' scalpels. Does my body remember? Did this first big shock begin rewiring my brain's chemical supply, serotonin receptors/release functions, and fight/flight/freak responses from the beginning?

I'd worked hard to seem normal, but with issues shelved for more than forty-five years, my mental vault was maxed and quickly crumbling. The plastic-princess persona realized that my emotional and spiritual capacity levels were at obvious breaking points.

In safe spaces encircled by safe people in stable, supportive environments with resources at my disposal, I was overwhelmed with gratitude, the cup of my soul warmed to the brim. The shiny fake facade dissolved, melting into a smooth plasticine pool on the floor. I looked down to behold a vaguely familiar face. *Who is she?*

Peering into my own distorted reflection—this real image without any camouflage—scared, surprised, then relieved me. Slightly repulsed, I was also strangely fascinated by Authentic Me.

Part of coming out of valley experiences requires unpacking and identifying those sealed boxes, but another issue has arisen. In the past, my brain boxed and shelved MOST memories, not just traumatic ones. Since this shelving method worked efficiently, I guess I kept it, unwilling to slow down or consider that while some events are horrifically vault-worthy, others are important and make me feel good to remember. Will I one day shine like a star in the universe holding both good and bad together firmly in Scripture-centered understanding and work out my salvation in awe and trembling, appreciating how God redeems it for His good purpose?

I sure hope so.

Cancer Sucks (06.26.2020)

Twenty-two days ago in my last trauma therapy appointment, another PTSD intrusive event detailed a fuller, more horrifying picture of what really happened in that Central American hotel room so long ago that I mentioned in chapter 2. That same Thursday, Christopher received an alarming text. The doctors informed the family our beloved matriarch, Sharon, would die sometime Saturday because of complications from an unexpected surgery. Within forty-eight hours, on June 6, 2020, the Mackenzie siblings became orphans.

Over the following weeks, blurred with tears, emotional voices, and more movement than I could possibly process, the six siblings and their families pushed tightly together, coordinating Mom's final hours of care and planning her COVID visitation and funeral. Each Mackenzie brought his or her A-game to the collective table to help the best they could. Our community and personal family friends delivered toilet paper, toiletries, and home-cooked meals to the front porch.

Sharon was like a mother to me, and her husband, Jack (who died eighteen months earlier), was a beloved father-figure.

The family liquidated belongings and prepared their family home for sale. Ten days after her funeral, it sold. Some immediately left to fulfill pressing responsibilities back home, while others remained at 1900 Jefferson Street under the roof of the house where we often celebrated Thanksgiving and Christmas together. They were gripped with the reality of being parentless on earth; if you've experienced it, you understand orphandom's aching desolation.

As executor of his parents' estate, Christopher plowed like a machine through an expanse of legal and financial paperwork. Trying to keep up, I did anything he needed, called whatever company or agency, all while battling my own grief, anxiety, and nightly panic attacks from the present stress and being triggered by the terror of that tropical night thirty-plus years ago.

Christopher still knew nothing of this most recent appalling PTSD attack or how it chased me, expanding my knowledge of that night, threatening to intrusively invade at any second. Unbearably stressed, I kept telling myself that I could not heap any more on my husband.

Except I did.

As we ran alongside one another through this "sprint" that life had suddenly wrought, I found myself angry and bitter. After ten days of overstimulation, irritation, and upset, my filter dissolved. Thoughts like, *If only I was raised in this family, I'd behave differently.* What's worse, I voiced these thoughts constantly as caustic verbal vomit that poisoned anyone in proximity. My husband and kids got to the place where they'd had it because one day, they told me so. My deep sins of unforgiveness, jealousy, and bitterness had to stop.

Holding on to offenses hurts the person holding them more than the one who caused them. As Lewis Smedes observed, "To forgive is to set a prisoner free and discover that the prisoner was you."[1]

Who was I to hold anything against anyone else? I had to forgive others' sin, though it affected my family and me, because I am certain my sin has affected others and their families too. In order for God to bring me into His family, my sin affected Jesus Christ. It's what put him on the cross, why God raised him in power and glory so I can live in forgiveness.

So, I confessed my unbelief, my faithlessness in God's well-being for me while bemoaning my childhood.

"If I could have been born in a family like Christopher's, if Sharon and Jack were my parents, Lord, just think how different my life would be! Why, Lord? Why didn't you give me a family like theirs? You could have if you wanted to." My fists clenched as I whispered these words through gritted teeth.

As I gazed over treetops in the steamy midwestern sun, sweat mingled seamlessly with salty tears rolling down my face and neck, absorbed by the dark band at my sweater's neckline. Had I ever given vent to this thought, this doubt, this challenge, so fully? With such ragged rawness and honesty, part of me felt vindicated for asking, the other part terrified I'd be struck dead for blasphemy.

Gah, this is such an ugly side of me, but even as I prayed, the Holy Spirit led me to this: *I have a beautiful life.*

My Father had given me everything—everything. Faith and family, a church and my children, health, and now healing. I wanted for nothing and wouldn't have traded this moment in time for a single second of anyone else's greatest glory days. Finally owning what was mine, I trusted God's power and purpose to transform me at my worst into something good.

Having lived in the spiritual gutter, I'm oh so grateful my Savior brings me into the holiest places, anoints my head with oil like a king and priest, and offers a seat at the table in the presence of enemies. My cup runneth over with His mercy and grace. Goodness and love have followed me all the days of my life. I will dwell in the house of the Lord forever (Psalm 23:5–6).

Again, I return to the hope found in the shepherd king's psalms:

> The LORD is my shepherd, I shall not be in want.
> He makes me lie down in green pastures,
> he leads me beside quiet waters,
> he restores my soul.
> He guides me in paths of righteousness
> for his name's sake.
>
> (Psalm 23:1–3 NIV84)

Verses to Consider

Psalm 23
Psalm 34:18
Psalm 46
Philippians 2:12–17

She Seems So Normal podcast

Chapter 8

RACEHORSES AND DANCING WITH THE D'EVIL

25

Digging to the Source of My Pain

It was never about the #@!%$ horse!

Forgive me. That sentence might seem offensive to those of a conservative, godly sensibility, but I gotta be real. A good expletive can truly mark a phrase appropriately. You cannot imagine my surprise and anger when I realized what I'm about to tell you. Although please note, I never wrote the actual cussword.

Enter: Dasanka.

Her proud white strip blazed down her face from forelock to fuzzy horse nose, and a single white sock emphasized this black beauty's perfect conformation. Since she was documented as American Quarter Horse Association Leo-line racehorse stock, her bloodline was an expensive commodity. True to her genetics, she was competitive and high-strung. She had been standing unridden in racetrack stalls for years after trainers initially broke her when my five-year-old self met her. She was challenging to control for any horseman.

My previous equestrian experience was at four years

old. My aunt rode with me on Christy Clay, an old race-horse at the end of her career. The big red horse trotted then galloped around the track as I clung to the saddle horn in terror, thinking, *Why can't horses just walk?*

Fast-forward one year.

With her sleek coat shining in the sun and fresh out of the trailer, Dasanka stomped her hooves majestically, creating clouds of dust in the corral. I'm not certain who decided to lift me up and put me into the saddle for the first time that day, but I bet I was thrilled to be so high up looking down at everyone . . . until Dasanka took off.

Sprinting through the gate, she swiftly turned a cor-ner and headed down the quarter-mile lane toward the highway, racing away from the barn. Terrified, scream-ing for help, I once again clenched a saddle horn for dear life. I relive these moments again now, the powerlessness, helplessness, my little soul strength drained tremendously, tired from the stress.

Dasanka deftly veered to one side, and Little Me flew through the air, landing feet from a concrete square that showcased a giant white propane tank, which always looked like a pig to me. Unable to rise, my hips and back hurting from the impact, I had difficulty walking. The joke is I was running around the hospital halls right after the exam and X-ray. They identified "nothing wrong" at the time, though later X-rays indicate an ancient broken place on my backbone, "probably from a big fall as a kid," the doctors explained after I was diagnosed with multiple ruptured discs and crippling pain in my twenties.

Why does my mind start with this "safe memory" for

my first EMDR session? No idea, but my brain quickly hops to another Dasanka story.

As we were going home late one night years after my rough ride, emergency lights flashed and sirens wailed down the highway toward exit 191. Slowly easing her blue Buick Skylark into the gravel, my mother stopped the engine. Through the backseat window, I recognized an unmoving equine body stretched across the north-bound lanes, a beautiful red chestnut beast we had been pasturing for a friend.

Movement caught my attention as another horse struggled on the highway's shoulder, hooves angrily kicking at air. Clambering out of the car onto the interstate, I immediately recognized her horse voice screaming as she tried to stand. Dasanka.

Her distress agitated me.

My mother shouted for my sister and me to gather up the remaining horses who had wandered off and lead them to our pasture's barbed-wire fence. The smell of gasoline and oil spilling out of an overturned sports car coupled with the exhaust from stopped cars made me sick to my stomach.

Then out of nowhere, the unmistakable sound of a gunshot. . . . The horse went still and silent.

Since she was beyond any hope of recovery, the state patrol officer mercifully put Dasanka out of her misery.

Sobbing, I walked the horses a quarter mile down another long gravel driveway. I wonder now how my sister and I ever got to sleep that night. Horse blood–stained asphalt and Dasanka's screaming, distressed shrieks haunted my nightmares for years.

The horse I feared and hated most of my young life died like this. We called her high-strung and a little dangerous, but the truth is, she was bred and groomed for it, always running, racing, pushing for first.

"I hated that horse," I told my therapist. "I wanted her dead, even prayed for her to die at times. She scared me." I felt horribly guilty, like somehow my wishing for Dasanka's death made it my fault.

Catching a glimpse of how I was raised, I actually became frustrated and more than a little upset. Would there be more memories coming? Or was this the worst it would get? I began to wonder, *Was it ever about the #@!%$ horse?* Or was it more about the family dynamics in which I was raised?

Why is it not about the horse? This critical memory allowed me to feel hate about the past. What I would find in future sessions were the many things I had stuffed into boxes throughout my young life, emotions I wasn't allowed to express, ones that were negated, chastised, or ridiculed.

Maybe you've already figured it out. The horse really isn't the evil in this story.

Returning to Little Me's first dangerous ride with Dasanka, I had many questions. Who put me on this unpredictable horse? There's no way in the world any five-year-old child of mine would be near this animal, let alone placed in a saddle five feet off the ground to ride with no one holding the reins for her.

Family lore is I begged to ride Dasanka first. I had no business ever riding a beast weighing over one thousand pounds that could have severely injured me or worse. The issue isn't that a five-year-old child couldn't control her horse, as it was laughingly claimed. Someone made the decision to place me on her back and I question why. Maybe I mistakenly hated the object (the horse) because, as a child, it was too dangerous to place anger and hate on anyone else—like the people in my life who directly or indirectly produced the real pain through their choices.

Know anyone who attaches feelings and memories to objects like I do?

I still can't recall most memories without prompts like photographs or jewelry because I pinned emotions on childhood objects, things, and circumstances. I guess Little Me and Middle Me refused to allow the blame and emotions to be attached to the people who were there. Mothers are supposed to be good, so I couldn't blame her. But what happens when parents make mistakes?

Instead of putting blame on people who earned it, I assigned it to places, objects, and myself. Self-disdain, self-criticism, and self-hate have been my regular hallmarks.

I wonder secretly, *Was I born to fail?*

Back to the Living Room with Little Me: The Fiends Who Masquerade as Friends

26

After speaking to spiritual mentors, the Holy Spirit again uncovered the evil at the root of it all. The spirits of bitterness, anger, rage, slander, malice, and hate plaguing me all began with jealousy and covetousness. Never before had I realized this. I prayed immediately to the Lord to make amends.

As I ended my confession, repentance, and renouncement of my sin, I was suddenly brought back to the living room of my mind where Little Me, Middle Me, and Teen Me reside. We sat once again on the green couch; Little Me was moaning in my arms, tears pouring down her face. I wrapped my arms around her, patting her back for comfort.

In real life, I wrapped my arms around myself and patted my own back.

"No, no, NO!" she wailed, shaking her head. She hit my shoulders as I pulled her closer to swaddle her.

"Little Me, we have to let them go. They are not our friends. They are the enemy," I told her calmly. She looked straight at me, her blue eyes almost an incandescent green against the redness of her skin and the rims of her eyes. Instinctively, I knew this was a vital space; I could not afford to become the child again. The tiny girl tilted her head, stopped crying, and wiped her nose across my chest, making a dark, shiny mark on my sky-blue sweater, reminding me of the same swipe of blood across her thigh so long ago in the Red Room.

Pushing the image from my mind, I could not understand why she didn't want these demons to leave. Then, I caught a glimmer of understanding: she's afraid of being all alone.

Why would she be alone?

Middle Me was there, sitting next to Grown-Up Me as Little Me continued to gulp and sniff. She listened to the entire conversation, as she always has.

"You don't have to be afraid," I said with confidence, "I am here. Your Father has given us everything. We do not need Jealousy and Covetousness anymore. We have everything we need, more than enough love. I'm your mother, and I promise nothing will ever happen to you again like that. You don't have to be jealous of anyone else anymore or want what others have."

As I gazed at Middle Me, my mind flashed to a

sleepover in elementary school with my best friend. As we sat around the dinner table, I caught my second-grade self wishing I could swap lives with her. I wished I lived with her family and had parents like her mom and dad. Her life seemed so perfect and so happy.

But just a few months later, her mother would be dead from cancer, and she would be left just as heartbroken and shattered as I was, just in a different way. Three lessons emerged from this realization.

Lesson 1: Everyone has a cross to carry. No one's life is as good as you think it is, no matter what their social standing appears to be or their social media shows. Everyone has a filter they use for the world to see them.

Lesson 2: The truth is, we all suffer in some way. It's just what we do with that suffering that is different.

Lesson 3: There is a cost for blessing, especially when it's a God-given gift, because we are blessed to be a blessing to others (Genesis 12:1–3).

Suddenly, in that moment, I realized my lifelong jealousy of other girls and women for one thing or another and my covetousness of what they had, whether it was family, faith, opportunity, or finances. Instead of Sally or Jane, my friends became Jealousy and Covetousness, and they made their home close to my heart long ago, crowding out many potential life-giving female relationships. They masqueraded as angels of light to comfort me, to keep my attention elsewhere—on despising and wanting other people's blessings—but they also kept me from friendships, real friendships with real people, not demons.

This realization hit like lightning and opened a watershed of understanding.

Bitterness, Anger, Rage, Malice, and Slander are good friends of Jealousy and Covetousness and joined up with Teen Me later in life as her coping methods became more advanced. I gasped and looked around the room for her. She, as usual, was standing, leaning against the doorjamb with her arms folded looking squarely at me. Her mouth was tight; her eyebrow raised.

"Come here, Child," I commanded. She obeyed reluctantly but came sooner than I expected. Putting my arms around her, I hugged her hard and close as I began to whisper in her ear loud enough for the other girls to hear.

"You! You are my warrior! You've been my defender! I am so proud of you; you are so strong. These . . . demons. They are *not* your friends. They are liars. They have deceived you. You think they have made you feel strong and important, but they have separated us from real humans who could actually help and strengthen us, who could be true friends.

"There is so much work to do, Teen Me. Stop living in the past; I need you here in the present for the assignment God has for us in the near future. We cannot waste time on lies. I need you. I need all of us together because this is the most important work of our lives.

"We have to let them go because they have hurt us more than most of the people around us. Say goodbye to them now and do not ever let them back into our life."

My entire body shook as I held her, holding on to myself and still patting my own back for comfort. As I verbally confessed, rebuked, renounced, and bound these evil spirits together in the name, power, and authority of Jesus Christ, I shuddered as I commanded them to go wherever my Lord and Savior would send them.

"And don't you dare come back ever again," I added quietly under my breath.

While I was at it, I also confessed and cast away the spirits of Misunderstanding, Death, and Infirmity from myself, my family, and my home and asked the Lord to send ministering angels to surround us.

Forgiveness, kindness, and compassion—everything begins and ends there. Paul writes in Ephesians 4:31–32: "Get rid of all bitterness, rage and anger, brawling and slander, along with every form of malice. Be kind and compassionate to one another, forgiving each other, just as in Christ God forgave you."

As much as I have wished to have someone else's opportunity, life, or family, I realize now that I am so grateful for who God created me to be. That "someone" is kind and compassionate and tries her best to be helpful. She strongly advocates for what she believes is right and good and works hard to promote it.

Sitting here now, in the coolness of my air-conditioned writing space, it occurs to me that I don't want to have what anyone else has. My life is more than blessed. I will press on, leaving behind the past, writing and encouraging boldly right now, knowing whose I am for all eternity.

> *I want to know Christ—yes, to know the power of his resurrection and participation in his sufferings, becoming like him in his death, and so, somehow, attaining to the resurrection from the dead.*
> *Not that I have already obtained all this, or have already arrived at my goal, but I press on to take hold*

*of that for which Christ Jesus took hold of me. Broth-
ers and sisters, I do not consider myself yet to have
taken hold of it. But one thing I do: Forgetting what
is behind and straining toward what is ahead, I press
on toward the goal to win the prize for which God has
called me heavenward in Christ Jesus.*

—Philippians 3:10–14

Verses to Consider
Psalm 23:4–5
Ephesians 4:31–32
Philippians 3
1 Peter 2:9–10
1 Peter 5:6–9

She Seems So Normal podcast

Chapter 9

28

ORIGIN OF MY SHATTERING

I waited patiently for the LORD;
he inclined to me and heard my cry.
He drew me up from the pit of destruction,
out of the miry bog,
and set my feet upon a rock,
making my steps secure.
He put a new song in my mouth,
a song of praise to our God.
Many will see and fear,
and put their trust in the LORD.

—Psalm 40:1–3 ESV

It has been a month from hell. I'm not kidding for a single moment.

As I write this, in the United States, we are at the beginning of the second spike in COVID-19 cases. Our communities have just opened up only to have to shut down again after three or four months of our very first pandemic quarantine.

My son's senior year has not been at all what we expected with virtual schooling, the cancellation of all senior traditions, and two quarantine graduation ceremonies. Stories of George Floyd, Breonna Taylor, and so many other injustices have set off riots across the country and around the world as well as more than a few fires in our little biracial family. We are all scrambling to find a fixed point on the horizon, and there's nowhere to look but upward to heaven. All of this reminds me just how broken our world is.

If it were only just that, except there will be so much more—more obstacles, more difficulties, more personal tragedies to unearth, more PTSD events, and more memories that I'll face.

The Box Is Opened and I Can't Close It (1.6.2020)

Healing comes when our story is raw, bone-deep and full of hunger for what only Jesus can offer.

—Dan B. Allender

It was January and the kids were finally back in school, though we didn't know at that point how the pandemic would totally change that in a matter of weeks. I was now deeply into the unpacking-my-life *shtick*, and it seemed to be going pretty well with one huge exception: I was constantly ragged and raw emotionally. I felt like a hopelessly knotted, entangled ball of yarn. Tears leaked out of my eyes at the silliest times; I was a mess and couldn't hold my "ish" together.[1] The plastic princess was starting to melt, and I couldn't figure out how to remake her like she was.

Can it be when you're working on putting your mind back together your life falls apart? The script that was replaying in my head was that I was no earthly good to anyone anymore if I couldn't pull it together like I used to. I had opened the box but possessed no solid resolution; I couldn't unsee what I had seen or unknow what I now knew. I couldn't put it back because there was too much left unhealed. I had come too far to stop, but I didn't know if there was any way I could move forward through this, and my next appointment wasn't for another week.

It was beginning to seem hopeless.

This valley was deep.

I was beginning to realize that there was so much work to be done for me to be well, and it was overwhelming. What if I never got better? What if I never got my ish together to function properly again?

What if we broke me?

At least before, though I was a mess, I was a highly functioning, helpful mess, kind of like a broken vase that was patched up and only leaked a little when you used it.

Now? Now I was a shattered vase with pieces all over the floor, completely unusable. Did everyone know it? I knew it. Places in the Scriptures reminded me of this, of being broken. My mind went to David:

> My sacrifice, O God, is a broken spirit;
>   a broken and contrite heart
>   you, God, will not despise. (Psalm 51:17)

While mankind may have looked with disappointment or disgust, I knew the Lord didn't despise my weakness.

Let's be honest though. Sometimes I despised me. I was so disappointed by what seemed like a total wreck of a life and disgusted with how pathetic I was. You cannot imagine the amount of self-loathing and hate I felt with myself at that very moment.

What happened to my carefully crafted facade that kept everyone out and thinking I was on top of the world? The perfect wife with the perfect life, living the dream with the perfect family, working in a perfect church. She had herself put together. People respected, even feared, her. She was intimidating, a bulldog at times. Do you need a room cleared? Let her at it. Do you need someone to take control and fix the problem? She's on it. But now she was broken and useless. Kick this weakling to the curb.

"Oh, God, I hate who I am right now! Please, let's go back to the other me."

Oh, wait, the one who was a fabrication, a painted mannequin, a complete lie—the plastic princess.

"I'm so tired of being her. I want to become who YOU say I am, Jesus. Help me become who you created me to be. Don't let me grow weary doing good. Don't turn your love and mercy away from me. You started this work; I know you will complete it . . . won't you?"

God didn't turn away because I was messy then. My heart was broken into so many tiny little shards because of the things that had happened as well as my own personal sinful reactions to them. Make no mistake, bad things had happened to me, but in response, I did bad things to others, myself, and ultimately to God Himself.

While there may be explanations, there is never an excuse for sin. Our only response is confession and true, godly repentance, which comes through the purifying work of the Holy Spirit.

> The Spirit of the Sovereign LORD is on me,
>   because the LORD has anointed me
>   to proclaim good news to the poor.

> He has sent me to bind up the brokenhearted,
>   to proclaim freedom for the captives
>   and release from darkness for the prisoners.
>
>   (Isaiah 61:1)

Lord, in Jesus Christ, bind me up; I need freedom and release from my chains. Make me whole again. Isaiah comforted me:

> For this is what the high and exalted One says—
>   he who lives forever, whose name is holy:
> "I live in a high and holy place,
>   but also with the one who is contrite and
>   lowly in spirit,
> to revive the spirit of the lowly
>   and to revive the heart of the contrite."
>
>   (Isaiah 57:15)

In late January 2020, Michele encouraged me from her vantage point, saying we'd almost reached the half-way point. Once we were through that, I would move to a cleanup phase, that I was at the climax of therapy. I didn't know walking into my therapist's room that day we would be entering the depths of sin and hell.

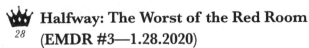 Halfway: The Worst of the Red Room (EMDR #3—1.28.2020)

My solo consolation every time I faced the terrifying past was something Michele kept reminding me: I. Was. Still. Standing. And God was there.

And she was right.

My therapist took me back to the Red Room. I had thought we were finished there, but no. The EMDR had waaaay more work to do with my brain and body to unearth why I had been so terrified of it.

Until December 2019, I hadn't thought of this room in years; my memories only danced around it. I had strange, conflicting feelings and emotions, but nothing I could pinpoint until then.

In my soul, I believe the Lord appointed a season of complete healing. I believe He shielded me from remembering this portion of my life until I held the faith, space, and support to face it lest I fracture into shards of glass all over again. A God of mercy and kindness, the Great Physician of righteousness and truth, He needed me to get to the center of why I am the way I am, why I have PTSD, anxiety, and depression, to mend me profoundly. All the significant glimpses of the Red Room forty days before were where He wanted me to start.

> *Yea, though I walk through the valley of the shadow of death, I will fear no evil: for thou art with me. Thy rod and thy staff, they comfort me. Thou preparest a table before me in the presence of mine enemies: thou anointest my head with oil; my cup runneth over.*
> —Psalm 23:4–5 KJV

Because this intrusive event is a trigger-fest for any child sexual assault or trafficking survivor or perpetrator of sexual abuse, I refuse describing it publicly or allowing these events to damage anyone else like they shattered five-year-old me. Make no mistake, I know how it happened, the man who did it, and that it's criminally despicable; decent men and women consider the vulgar actions of child rape unforgivably treacherous.

However, I will disclose that after discovering the depth of wickedness that happened to me, I was terrorized for days by the thought of any man being near me. I felt no man or woman was safe or trustworthy anymore. I feared being near anyone except prayer sisters or my daughter.

 ### The Broken Pot (Jeremiah 18:1–4)
30

In this season I've begun to have a different perspective on broken things. Jeremiah 18 describes a potter who keeps reshaping the clay until the pot is just right, symbolizing God's work in Israel. God is the potter, and we are the clay.

This story and my own brokenness have helped me identify with Japanese art during this season of healing. It's as if God has been preparing me to see something important through it.

Wabi sabi. One website says wabi sabi is "the elusive beauty of imperfection."[2] The wabi sabi practice of *kintsugi* mends broken porcelain with liquid gold glue, creating art pieces that are worth far more than they were before they were broken. There are galleries of priceless broken-mended bowls, vases, cups, and pots crafted by artisans who saw beauty in imperfection, incompleteness, and impermanence.

Someday, will God complete His work in me? Will He mend all the broken and cracked pieces together so I can be of greater value to His kingdom? Can I accept there is no perfection here, that it's only in Christ? Maybe at the end of this beautiful journey, I will accept the imperfect, impermanent, and incomplete parts of me.

There is beauty to be seen in brokenness.

Verses to Consider

Psalm 51:17
Psalm 88
Isaiah 61:1
Jeremiah 18:1–4

She Seems So Normal podcast

Chapter 10

RESTORING IDENTITY

Parents and Babies

There's a powerful video called "Still Face Experiment" by Dr. Edward Tronick.[1] Demonstrating interactions between a mother and her one-year-old daughter, the documentary begins with the mother greeting her infant; the baby girl delightedly responds. Moving on to touch, then more talking, when the tiny girl points, the mother responds, looks, and talks to her daughter about what she sees. "They're working to coordinate their emotions and intentions and what they want," Dr. Tronick says.

In stage two, researchers ask the mom to have no response. As the baby picks up on this, she quickly begins employing all her primitive skills to reengage her mother. But the mother's face stays blank (at this point in the video, I began sobbing, watching the distress of the child's reactions). Hands go up to her face, she screeches and shrieks, in effect trying to communicate, "Mommy! Why aren't you responding to me? This isn't good!"

As the mother reengages, her child calms, and they begin to play again. The baby is restored to her formerly calm state; they move forward, restoring and reconciling the rift quickly.

What I realized from this demonstration is that a baby is a baby and it's a parent's responsibility to parent. And a baby's identity is thoroughly wrapped up in her relationship to her mother. I've felt profoundly rejected or forsaken by both of my parents throughout the years.

You might say, "Well, who hasn't?"

I always wondered what was wrong with Little Me. Did I do something to deserve these feelings of rejection and abandonment?

What about you? Have you ever wondered too? Has your identity been tied to behavior? If I behaved better, maybe daddy would stay and not hurt mommy, my siblings, or me. If only I was a good little girl, mommy would feed me supper and not drink, do drugs, be with that bad man, or hit me. Will they pay attention if I excel academically, step up my style, lyrically harmonize, or score the winning point? With more bravery, strength, or courage, could I stand up to the different monsters in my life that I can never please?

What Grown-Up Me learned is it never had anything to do with me. *It never had anything to do with you either, Child.*

Loss and pain caused by complicated, grown-up issues affect us as children. The sins of the parents affect their offspring. Were those entrusted to care for us also themselves neglected, groomed, or abused by the previous generation? When destructive family behavior systems perpetuate dysfunction, hurt people exponentially hurt many people, not just me.

Not just me.

At some level, trauma survivors share pain from

the past and are often tempted to think that we are different from everyone else. However, God gave us the remedy: learning the reality of our identity in Christ. Our Christian identity trumps everything in our past. *Everything.* For this identity to be active in our lives, we need faith to believe that what Scripture says about us is true.

Recapping this first trauma therapy session:

- Babies are born to be cared for and loved. There are no expectations of a baby except to eat, poop, sleep, snuggle, and then start all over again.

- Fault lies at the feet of those who hurt or don't protect children; sin hurts everyone.

- You can't love someone and expect love back if it's not in their capacity to do so.

- The wounds we have are so deep only the blood of Jesus fills them and makes us whole again.

This session also highlighted how vital my identity in Christ is. It assured me:

- There was never anything wrong with me in the first place. (Can I get a "Hallelujah!"?)

- No person stands in the gap for our healing or makes us feel accepted except the Savior Himself.

I remain confident of this: I will see the goodness of the
LORD in the land of the living. Wait for the Lord;
be strong and take heart and wait for the LORD.
—Psalm 27:13–14

♔ Hold On

32   I was talking to a dear, close friend (one who has walked with the Lord for years), and she confided to me that even when she is in the middle of a huge crowd with people all around her in church, she feels totally cut off and alone. Imagine, in the place where we should feel the greatest fellowship and Spirit-filled quenching, we are dry and parched in our isolation.

I have felt the exact same way. Identity must constantly be remembered because we so easily forget.

Appearing to be everything to everyone on the outside, I have been a barren wasteland on the inside, the sand kicking up and swirling across miles and miles of desert. Only an occasional tumbleweed or snake would break up the blistering scene. When I am consumed by my fears, hurts, or sadness, I tend to isolate, effectively cutting myself off from the help I could have within the body of believers.

"I am all alone."

This week in the news were two notable suicides— fashion designer Kate Spade and TV personality chef Anthony Bourdain. They left families, friends, and fans behind in the wake of their choices.

For many people, it's hard to understand how you can go so low to the point of killing yourself. Not for me.

It's the battlefield of the mind and soul.

Where do we focus? "Finally, brothers, whatever is true, whatever is honorable, whatever is just, whatever is pure, whatever is lovely, whatever is commendable, if there is any excellence, if there is anything worthy of praise, think about these things" (Philippians 4:8 ESV).

Blogging at thechurchgirlwrites.com, I wrote a dark creative meditation called "Don't Let Go" about a little girl. In this fictional story, I describe a child left alone in a cave realizing nothing could save her from the surrounding darkness except one man. Here it is.

Don't Let Go (June 1, 2018, from my blog, *The Church Girl Writes*)

29

Tear-stained eyes, bright and wide open, cast about the darkened cavern nervously. Shadows make monsters on every wall. Drips of water sound like thunder in the silence.

"Is there any . . . body . . . h-h-here?"

Her tiny voice whispers, then quietly echoes into the space, bouncing off wet bedrock walls and stalactites. Hugging herself closely, she huddles in the corner, cold and wet. The threadbare cotton tunic is stained with unmentionable filth and muck; through the holes, the scars are readily apparent on her skeleton frame.

"I am all alone. No one can save me now." The realization hits hard; her entire body begins to shake furiously.

Her face reddens and grimaces; the little lips press tightly together to try to hold in the cry that will eventually escape in a force of pent-up emotions. Hot tears come fast and furiously, though she presses dirty fingers into her eyes to stop the flow. The ugly, muffled moan of terror begins.

All hope is lost. No one is coming. Ever.

Darkness envelops, swirling around her and taking her deep, deep into the abyss.

Suddenly, a soft light warms the cave and moves slowly toward the little girl. A gentle voice issues from it.

"Are you here, Little One? I've been searching for you." The voice is lyrical and reaches her ears, drawing her into the light on all fours. There is a man dressed in white standing close by. Looking up through ratted locks of hair, she dares to steal a look at his face. His eyes are so bright, they are like fire. She shields her eyes, turning her head to the side. Though his face is glowing white, she immediately trusts the hand that reaches out to her.

"I've come for YOU. Take my hand and I'll help you."

The back of her dirt-encrusted forearm wipes the snot from her nose. She dares to have hope, to wonder if this is real. She inches forward only to see the scars on his feet first.

"What are those?" His presence gives her the courage to ask.

"Those were for you and for those who have hurt you," he replies, squatting down to her level. "Although your mother and father and others have forsaken you, I receive you, Dear Child. You are mine." Holding his hands out, he beckons her to come to him.

"What are these?" She points to the scars on his wrists, the shiny silver-gold flesh glinting as the light hits it.

"These were the cost of your freedom, Beloved. It's how I was able to find you to bring you home to me." She looks once again and can now see the man through all the fire and light. His face is tender, eyes soft, mouth smiling. He seems familiar and safe and trustworthy.

"Come to me. You are weary. I will give you rest."

The moment she touches him, she is transformed. Warmth floods her entire body as if she has been immersed in water. Looking down at her hands, they are supple and clean, not a spot of dirt is left under her fingernails. She gazes in wonderment down at herself, finding her filthy smock is now brand-new, white as snow, and soft against her freshly cleaned skin. Her hair no longer a tangled veil, she reaches up to touch it and finds soft ringlets of curls that feel like silk between her fingers.

"I make all things new," he says looking into her questioning eyes. "You never have to fear again. You have a new future and never have to return here again."

As she stands up, she feels his strength flooding into her frame, like light from the brightest star filling her entire body. She stands to her feet and shyly smiles into his kindly face.

"I'm ready," she says, grasping his hand tightly.

"I will lead you. Follow me and don't let go."

In stories like this I am reminded of my identity in Christ.

This came as a vivid vision for me. By the end of the piece, "hope" comes for the little girl, and His name is Jesus.

I wonder if both Kate and Anthony felt like they were in that cave before they decided on a permanent solution for temporary problems. I pray that they had interacted with believing Christians before their passing and accepted Jesus Christ before the end. I pray for peace for their families and that good will somehow come from these tragic stories.

Can we let go of the past and let the love of Christ be our rock-solid foundation? The irony is that when we don't let go of our fears, hurts, and sadness, we have no hope for our future but are held captive by our lack of trust in God and our unwillingness to forgive others. d'Evil is a thief.

We consign ourselves to living in the dark, overcome by isolation and loneliness, where the enemy blacks out our lives and relationships physically, emotionally, and spiritually. He holds us captive in our lack of trust in God and our unwillingness to forgive others. He is a thief that seeks to kill, steal, and destroy relationships (John 10:10), primarily our relationship with God. What is it we are missing? What part of God's character are we not believing? Who have we not forgiven? What are we holding on to?

If you struggle here, please read this and let it soak into the depths of your heart and soul:

> He will never leave you or forsake you.
> He will be your rock and your protector,
>   your safe harbor, your place of rest.
> Jesus fights for you, cares for you in your times
>   of need, and He never will throw you away
>   or leave you, no matter what.

He has good plans for your future.
He wants you so badly to find the freedom
His death and blood paid for you when He
    forgave you and all mankind to set you free
    from your fears, your hurts, and your sadness
    because His perfect love casts out all fear.
What are we holding on to?
Who are we listening to?
Who are we trusting in?
"Follow me. Take my hand and don't let go."
    We're not alone when we struggle.

Ephesians 2:8–10 says, "For it is by grace you have been saved, through faith—and this is not from yourselves, it is the gift of God—not by works, so that no one can boast. For we are God's handiwork, created in Christ Jesus to do good works, which God prepared in advance for us to do."

So why was I still trying to find my identity through works? No idea—just that the enemy loves to twist the truth around, and maybe I was trying to prove my worth to those who looked like me—the other plastic people. I just wanted to "get it right" and blend.

Paul goes on to talk about "the dividing wall of hostility" between Jews and Gentiles (v. 14), how previously there were "innies" and "outies" of faith and promises. Clearly, I kept assuming I would forever remain an "outie."

Ephesians 2:12–13 says, "Remember that at that time you were separate from Christ, excluded from citizenship . . . foreigners to the covenants of the promise, without hope and without God in the world. But now in

Christ Jesus *you who once were far away have been brought near by the blood of Christ*" (emphasis mine).

Grappling with these mind-blowing thoughts, I realize now that I have been brought near by the blood, not by the works. I have not been pushed outside the circle of hope and grace, but brought near and embraced by the love of the Father.

Verses to Consider

The Bible gives many statements about our identity:

We are justified and not guilty of sin (Romans 3:24).
No condemnation awaits (Romans 8:1).
We are set free from the law and death (Romans 8:2).
We are made holy and acceptable through Christ
     (1 Corinthians 1:2).
We are right before Jesus (1 Corinthians 1:30).

She Seems So Normal podcast

Chapter 11

POWERED BY PICKLE JARS
AND FAMILY SUPPORT

What would your nearest and dearest be willing to do for your healing journey? Mine hugged, high-fived, and helped me smash glass. How far was the Father willing to go to save our souls? He sent His Son as the perfect sacrifice and raised him up for our victory.

God is our refuge and strength, always ready to help in
times of trouble.
—Psalm 46:1 (NLT)

I've only been on my trauma therapy recovery journey since December 2019. As I edit this manuscript today, it's mid-May in 2022, and I can't believe how far and fast I've traveled down the road to healing. For forty-seven years, I did everything I knew to try to heal myself. Until the origins of my issues were unearthed and exhumed piece by piece, I limped and stumbled, unable to reconcile or understand anything without unlocking these repressed childhood memories. I credit the Holy Spirit's power to heal me through God's Word and His working through all the people supporting me along the way. Be encouraged and empowered that any abuse or trauma survivor could find healing so quickly.

As a "momma bear" kind of mom, I am constantly watchful over my children and on guard against evil. Imagining parents incapable of caring for or refusing to care for their child's needs confounds me. Parents are supposed to know best, do what's right, and always have their child's interests at heart.

Whether or not my mom was complicit or knew anything that happened, memories from Dasanka the runaway horse and the other disturbing tavern and hotel scenes all make me question my own mom's parenting priorities and perspectives. What I realize looking back is we were *all* groomed and programmed to behave certain ways by my predatory abusers. But at this moment in time, with my mind split between Little, Middle, and Teen Me because of the horrific abuses by men at such tender ages, Grown Me is finally enraged enough to begin asking questions.

Is it sinful for us as Christians to feel rage toward others or muster deep, visceral, primordial indignation for those who enable or allow hurt and abuse? Or is it worse to misplace anger, allowing it to land on others who are innocent?

Michele suggested the following glass smash process as a method to physically get in touch with and find an outlet for my repressed fury using a safe, tangibly representative outlet. Punching bags instead of people, yelling at inanimate objects representing the trauma versus verbally abusing your besties, or shooting arrows at paper abuser targets instead of aiming barbs at your associates—pick your poison and use whatever floats the boat. For me, the exquisite feel and sound of shattering delicate glass and china while voicing every hidden question about my hurt was cathartic and exceptionally more productive and less expensive than breaking farmhouse windows.

Today Is the Day (Saturday—2.15.2020)

54

My daughter told me, "I love you. You got this. Give me a high five!" as I headed into the garage. Earlier she and Christopher had surrounded me in a group hug— our form of love and prayer. My son, Julian, was still asleep from his drama production last night, but I knew he had been praying too.

You cannot understand how much I hated these memories of racehorses and Red Rooms, of predators with stubbled chins on glass shards while at the same time holding completely devastating sadness. *Where was my mom in all of this?* That had been one of my most feared and difficult unanswered questions.

Repeatedly throughout this stage of healing I had wanted to turn everything on myself, all the rage and hurt, to protect my mom and others who stole parts of my life from me. Teen Me wanted to slash my hands with her fingernails and carve my arms with glass.

Why did Teen Me feel like turning the knife on me? I didn't do anything wrong.

As I stepped onto the concrete floor, chills ran through my entire body. The tears had been falling all morning in anticipation of finally unleashing this anger. My gentle soul didn't want to be mad at anyone, but a necessary part of healing is recognizing who hurt me and how the displaced and misguided anger fits, instead of it spilling sideways onto those we love most when they least expect it. For heaven's sake, *I* never knew when to expect it! Triggers were once invisible, but my eyes had been unveiled to the wiles and ways of how the enemy tried to destroy my family and me.

No more.

When something went wrong, I used to put others on a pedestal, reasoning it was my fault. Making false idols, I placed those who seemed untouchable atop the altar of my mind and heart. I ended up worshipping them, yet sacrificing my husband and children, venting anger sideways because they were safest, because they unconditionally loved me.

> Courage never takes away fear; courage simply redistributes fear to get the job done.
>
> —Dan B. Allender, *Leading with a Limp*

The gravest danger of unresolved, misdirected anger for me is passing sinful, ungodly relationship behaviors down to the next generation's spouses, children, and their children. While God promises blessings to a thousand generations of those who are obedient and love the Lord, the sin of the father goes down to the fourth generation. And so, dysfunctional sin cycles continue, generation after generation.

> You shall not make for yourself an image in the form of anything in heaven above or on the earth beneath or in the waters below. You shall not bow down to them or worship them; for I, the LORD your God, am a jealous God, punishing the children for the sin of the parents to the third and fourth generation of those who hate me, but

showing love to a thousand generations of those who love me and keep my commandments. (Deuteronomy 5:8–10)

Who will stand up to stop it?

In the corner I saw the box of glasses and china I purchased from the thrift store for this very occasion to vent my anger, ask the hard questions, and shatter things. As I dragged the cardboard box into the center of the garage next to a metal trash can lined with heavy paper, Bella reminded me to wear safety glasses to protect my eyes. Christopher provided thin leather gloves to protect my hands from shards, but I decided against them—I needed to feel it all.

Half-heartedly, I tossed the first wine glass, a heavy, ugly, thick-stemmed number. It refused to break, so I picked it up and slammed it in the bottom of the trash can. Nope. Apparently, there was technique to this smashing; the paper was too cushioning. Irritated this wasn't working as I had imagined, I whipped the glass against the side of the can with all my strength and heard a lovely *p-sssshhhh!* as it broke.

Satisfying. The sound wave traveled to my hypersensitive ears, stimulating fight-or-flight in my brain. Immediately, I knew I was taking a stand to fight.

Here's what I realized. I'd

- never been really mad for real things,
- shielded people from blame and accountability,
- always made excuses for what happened to me,
- protected the miserable past at the expense of the miraculous present,

- tried to make people proud while feeling like a failure, and
- done what others wanted me to even when it pierced my soul to do them.

Am I betraying family by disrupting the past?

It may seem like it, but if there is anything I have realized through my time in therapy, it's that we need to place the right emotions in the right places and allow the Spirit to heal. By not paying attention to and caring for gaping emotional and spiritual wounds, while we pick at scabs or play with oozing pus, we continue to suffer instead of becoming whole and healed with help. We choose to limp along in life.

My wounds had festered far too long.

That day in the garage, the parasympathetic response to fight released a ton of pent-up hormones and emotions and gave me the strength to muster the anger of injustice I had buried so long. I focused in like a laser beam on the details—something trauma survivors master is swirling in the details.

I began asking:

Why wasn't I protected?

Was I ever loved?

How could this happen?

Why did you do nothing?

Didn't you love me?

What happened to you to let you think this was OK?

Did you know?

Didn't I deserve better?

Why did Dad leave? When?

Where was God in all of this?

These sound like childish questions as I am writing this, but they came from the child within me who was hurt so deeply so long ago. With every glass smash, the anger deepened as the sound rang through the garage. Sobbing, sloppy questions poured forth. Oftentimes with incoherent groans, grunts, and cries, I became animalistic in sound, blinded by tears.

It was utterly cathartic and pleasing. In the physical throwing and smashing, it was as if every fiber in my body that contained pressurized anger finally released on a target, a proper target. Whoosh. Hearing the glass break felt freaking awesome, and pouring out sorrow into that trash can unleashed my deepest, most honest and feared questions.

Reaching down to resmash a plate that didn't shatter as expected, my knuckles grazed wineglass splinters on metal. Recoiling with a snarl, I examined the blood that was beginning to bloom across the cracks of my skin.

"I will NOT be hurt by this. I REFUSE to be hurt anymore!" I brushed the tiny shards off and applied pressure to the cut; my blood obeyed and refused to rise to the surface.

The glass smash continued, but I was becoming exhausted and the garage was freezing. The outside temperature was −4 degrees. Warming myself by the portable heater plugged into the wall gave me a chance to reset and refocus.

As the box of thrift store items dwindled and expired, I was far from finished. Realizing I had run out of available options, I tentatively knocked on the door for Christopher.

"Yes, Baby?" Christopher answered, "Are you doing OK?"

"There's no more glass. I need more glass," I said, blubbering.

I watched as his mind moved into action. He smiled. "Hold on. I think I can help."

As I waited, my toes were freezing inside my thin blue canvas Chuck Taylors. Smiling for a moment, the broadcast stylist in me asked sarcastically, *Really, what DO you wear for this kind of thing?* Today it was sweatpants, a large black sweatshirt, and a pink cable-knit ski hat. Not one of my best outfits, I suppose, but it was highly practical.

The door opened slightly. Christopher nimbly, gently announced, "Um, here you go, Leigh-Leigh."

The man offered a clean empty pickle jar, which I smashed promptly. Other pickled condiment jars showed up outside the door—jars from giant capers, mini capers, bread-and-butter pickles, dill spears—and when the empty jar of his favorite salsa appeared, I knew he earnestly meant business. As my mind wondered where he was putting the contents of these jars, I laughed. How had God blessed me with this husband of mine? Even as I ran out of glass, with more questions persisting, demanding smashing responses, Christopher supplied the means for me to finish asking while God provided me with answers. I smashed everything he offered.

Residual anger lingered, still needing an outlet, but my gratitude grew knowing that: I. Was. Still. Standing.

Searching through storage cabinets hanging in the garage, I found fine wedding china and stemware, long-forgotten, unused, etched wine goblets, and champagne glasses found at a long-ago yard sale.

As I fingered the gold-leaf rings painted onto delicate blue 1960s cordial glasses, I realized these might have appeared in black-and-white family photos in my parents' hands. It was an incomplete set with only five remaining; my mother gave them to me decades ago when Christopher and I were married. Would I dare to break these precious glasses my parents loved and valued so highly?

Yes.

Before beginning, I mourned their loveliness, thinking how shattered they would be. The sweet, high-pitched *p-sssshhhh!* of the expensive fine glass breaking was music to me. With each glass shattered, I proclaimed . . .

God has been with me (*psshoow!*) (Romans 8:31).

Jesus has never forsaken me (*ching!*) (Deuteronomy 31:6).

The Lord is my stronghold (*chssshhh!*) (Psalm 27:1).

He is my safe place (*chitinnnnsh!*) (Psalm 46:1).

I will not be shaken (*keeeesseuw!*) (Psalm 16:8).

And instead of feeling empty and sad, I was strengthened with resolve and conviction.

My God walked me through the valley of the shadow of death, His hand in mine, leading me along the path so many times. He never left my side. Even before I knew him as Lord and Savior, my King spread out His arms between heaven and earth on a cross to rescue my soul from the pits of hell, out of the grip of evil men and the claws of the d'Evil! He loved me through eternity, and my name is written on the palm of His hand. I will not be stolen out of His grip! My Rescuer knew these days of freedom were coming in this exact season, and He appointed all the days of my life since before He laid the foundations of the earth. There is nothing too hard or impossible for Him.

That wasn't what I designed for you. I'm sorry
(deeply grieved) that happened to you—however—I
will use it to create something beautiful in you.
Trust me.

—God

The Lord gave this message to Michele to share with me at the beginning of the journey. After writing it on the back of a to-do list for her housekeeper, she sent it to me in the mail because I wanted evidence to remind me of it in the coming months. The truths I'm trusting and holding on to about God are threefold:

1. He did not design me for destruction.
2. He is sorry.
3. He will redeem it all.

The Ancient of Days never ordained the atrocities that happened. I was never a throwaway child fit for destruction or marked for abuse, though the enemy tried his best to deceive me into believing those lies. What happened to me and so many others was the work of man's free will and the evil in a fallen world. The enemy prompts temptation and mankind believes in satisfying his selfish, sinful urges in his staunch refusal and rebellion to trust in God's plan.

I am a child of God and no longer a slave to fear or these fits of rage and anger. I am a daughter of the King.

It's remarkable how far glass flies when it's shattered. As I swept up into a large industrial dustpan the little pieces of glass that had somehow escaped the trash can, I thought, *This was highly productive.*

So ended the glass smash. I'm thankful for the power of pickle jars and family support, aren't you?

I need some lunch now . . . and a nap.

Verses to Consider

Deuteronomy 31:6
Psalm 16:8
Psalm 27:1
Psalm 46:1
Romans 8:31

She Seems So Normal podcast

Chapter 12

WARPING THE IMAGE OF GOD

Food as a Weapon, a Mannequin Manifested

It was mid-May 2020, and I was turning forty-nine the next week. The world, our leaders, the new laws, the face mask debate, how the virus was spreading . . . nothing was straightforward, certain, or stable. It was driving me bananas, and that wasn't a far drive after more than sixty days in lockdown. We were glasses filled to the brim just waiting to spill what was inside onto the table or all over everyone else.

As the quarantine raged on in our state, I perceived low- to mid-level anxiety inside and around me. My daughter was sick of the day-to-day obnoxiousness of living in a space under 1,600 square feet with three other family members who were breathing and living too loudly for her sensitive sensibilities. My son was constantly online with his friends playing video games until late in the night. Christopher was in "nothing's really changed" mode because, as an essential worker in finance, nothing really had changed in his world. I was annoyed and feeling caged. Even though I am an introvert homebody, life in such a close space was getting on my nerves and under my skin. How was I dealing with it?

I defaulted to an age-old primitive coping mechanism: I stopped eating. I didn't even realize it.

That was the way I remained in control when everything else was out of control as a teenager.

As if it hadn't been enough for me to discover the past and heal my mind and soul, God was true to His word of wanting to heal me completely. He was even moving on such a profound level as to affect my body image.

See, I am a recovering anorexic, bulimic, and laxative addict. In the distant past, I was a serial psycho weight analyzer, stepping on the scale up to twenty times a day to check whether or not I had gained or lost ounces. You read that correctly—ounces.

There. I wrote it.

Once again, I was fighting the shame welling up inside of me.

I wonder what it will be like to have these words come out of my mouth one day. I wonder if they ever will. It's a lot easier to write them than to say them because to hear my own voice confessing this aloud would mean announcing it to the world. Right now, this is just a draft of my narrative, so I can take the words back anytime by simply highlighting them and deleting them.

But it's time to be honest about this . . . even this.

THIS.

(I stopped writing this to pray because I don't even know how to tackle something so big. The motivation for an entire sickening lifestyle of bondage, it's also *my* part in the story, *my* response to my childhood.)

I became obsessed with food, calories, and overexercising the year I got my period and began to look like a woman. Before then, starvation or hyper-analysis of food never occurred to me. I happily ate whatever I wanted and ran around like a child.

(Present-day note: Witnessing the blossoming of a girl into a young lady with my own beautiful daughter, I am overjoyed. Celebrating and honoring this milestone for her, I welcome her into the circle of WOMAN. There are things I want to teach and help her with as she maneuvers the amazing changes that God has blessed [and cursed!] us with as the fairer sex who give life to the image of God in the human race.)

For myself, however, I never celebrated, only hated. Despising the changes that brought me into woman-hood, especially the widening hips, fuller belly, and grow-ing chest, I did whatever I could to somehow cut away what I considered "fat" and "ugliness" to try to get back to my child body.

Until now, it never made sense why I hated my body so much. Now it seems so clear.

It was him.

As soon as I showed signs of puberty and growing up, his countenance slowly turned against me. I was demoted from the position of "most favored" as he spoke with disgust to me about how I looked. These were some of the worst, most caustic years of my life. He hated how I'd grown into a woman and was never ashamed to let me know it.

While he planted and watered the seeds of distortion, others tended that garden too. From glamour magazines showcasing heroin-chic mannequins like Kate Moss to the fad diets that were lifted up on morning television, in the eighties and nineties when I grew up, bony was con-sidered beautiful. However, one "gardener" surprised me on a beach in Puerto Rico.

"You never used to have all that belly fat."

The sun smiled down and waves crashed as her voice reached my ears. As I got out of the water after frolicking with my kids and husband, I remember my mom pointing to my forty-something paunch beneath the tankini I had carefully chosen for this trip. "We should do something about that. Let's go on a diet when we get home."

Maybe she didn't mean it like I received it, but her words pierced like a familiar blade.

Never before had I tied my anorexia and body dysmorphia to sexual abuse.[1] Now I understand the underlying belief behind my eating disorders. My childhood body, not my grown one, pleased the child molesters and pedophiles. In a sick, twisted way, these eating disorders were subconscious programming messages from my abusers; the "groomer" portion still resides in me like poison reinfecting me every time I look in the mirror.

Teen Me reasoned that if she could look like she did as Little and Middle, he wouldn't be so mean and treat her as "nicely" as he did before she grew breasts and hips and became desirable for other men. When it didn't work, no matter how hard she tried, Teen Me became angry. She wanted to throw knives, honestly, to cut him down and kill his thoughts in her head, but they always missed the mark, ricocheting to hit her.

Around that time of puberty, I became desperate to disappear and desperate for control. I often fantasized of simply vanishing. So, I stopped eating. This was the way the enemy could carve into the image of God—by distorting a young woman's view of her God-given looks each time she saw herself.

This is when suicide—real disappearing—became

a regular fantasy. It was my way out if things ever got too bad.

There was no one to shield me; no one to help. I was on my own and would never have told a teacher or counselor. Could you imagine my shame if they found out about my crazy home life—the alcoholism, how I had every bar phone number memorized from calling around to find the "adults" in my life.

Or the abuse. I would have never breathed a word about the abuse.

Diet soda and tortilla chips became my sustenance at home and the double chocolate chip cookies purchased from the lunch line kept me going in junior high. Sometimes I would binge and then feel so guilty, so out of control, that I would purge as much as I could. One time I ate a half of a corned beef brisket and then vomited stringy red masses until it was gone, or maybe I was too exhausted to keep going. I learned the foods that were awful coming back up a second time and the ones that weren't so bad and began tailoring how I would binge and purge.

Then there were the laxatives I carefully cultivated with my other methods. It seemed a little more sophisticated to take pills, but soon I was taking so many I began telling people I had a weak stomach. Ashamed to be seen buying so often, worried the gas station clerk was catching on, I stole a pack from the shelf, putting money in its place.

Can you believe how desperate you become when you believe in a lie? However ashamed I feel, I pray my story encourages others to get help.

Living out of abuse with the sad little tools I had at my disposal, this method raised its ugly head even after I was married. When I was feeling stressed, slighted, or abandoned, I occasionally vowed to punish myself or Christopher by not eating.

After accepting Christ, I felt more equipped and had a handle on it. Believing the power of Jesus Christ could set me free from the sin and death of eating disorders, I was marginally free, but I couldn't contemplate mastery until I understood the root seed, the actual lie and thought, from whence it stemmed. These seed lies are thoughts I captured and demolished to annihilate strongholds and anything else that went against my identity in Christ. The divine weapons of God's truth and the Holy Sprit's powerful wisdom steadfastly remain at our disposal for vanquishing behaviors meant to destroy us.

Ask me about the Christian discipline of fasting, and I'll tell you it is a no-brainer, though with my history I have to be careful. With quarantine lockdown pressure-cooking mankind, my family, and me, this issue raised its ugly head again.

What is your default under stress?

To this day, major stress still sends me backsliding into food abstinence, except now it's sneakier. Instead of being a conscious thought, it's an insidious, unconscious reaction. I don't know I am doing it and forget to eat if food doesn't sound appetizing.

Approaching my fifth decade, I've found my body doesn't bounce back as readily and certainly doesn't look like it did at a younger age. Preferring hipbones, ribcages, jawlines, and clavicles instead of curves, when I look in the mirror, fleshy parts of my body still sometimes disgust me.

It's hard to write or speak about this because victory is yet off in the distance peeking over the horizon. However, like all my issues, this one requires trusting Jesus to show His version of beauty for me. It's going to be hard, but healing is coming, though it still seems so painfully far away.

Plastic-Princess Deconstruction

Why did I finally seek help, knowing the price of change is pain?

Before, I never loved or cared for myself enough to voluntarily seek therapy or help. I decided to seek help only when I realized how much damage I was causing my tween daughter and teen son from what I perceived, spoke, and thought about myself, from my anger flares, undetected anxiety, and panic attacks, and my out-of-control parenting. I was causing them anxiety! Author and speaker Brené Brown says anxiety is highly contagious, and I know she's right.[2] I realized I couldn't do that to my kids anymore. I might not have loved myself, but as a mother, I certainly wanted better for them.

Though the road was arduous and filled with tears (both of sadness and joy), depression, anxiety panic attacks, and intrusive PTSD events, I believe a wall of mighty war angels surrounded me. Monumental wins coupled with few soul-crushing losses. Childhood sexual abuse is the ultimate betrayal, but healing from it becomes a tale of tremendous bravery for many as we lend courage to others to persevere, even while scared, and trust in the yoke of God's goodness and His greatness over the course of a lifetime.

I just wanna let you know something. You sit in the front row to a narrative through the valley of the shadow of death that has unfolded as I've written, so I hope the ending is just as surprising to you as it was for me.

The following theme is one I keep repeating, and it is the ending of the entire narrative: I. Am. Still. Standing.

God never left me, nor has He forsaken me. He will never leave you, even if you don't know Him. He is faithful. I am praying that what's contained in this manuscript somehow plants seeds that grant you the strength and peace to grow a tree of healing for you and those you love most.

Here's another moment of complete transparency:

- At parts too terrifying to endure, I thought I was gonna die—like, really die-die and leave this earth.
- The waters got so rough, they threatened to drown me, and in places I would have crumbled, I held on for dear life to my Rock, my God.
- You have no idea how badly I want to quit therapy because unearthing dead bodies to expose necrotic decay hurts, but the consequence of leaving them decaying hurts infinitely worse.

Yet, the Holy Spirit helped me always, providing unexpected people, medical professionals, prayer warriors near and far, and spiritual armor as He answered my cries and confirmed each step through my lowland times. By His power, we have the courage to understand our origin stories and change our victim mentality into a victory reality.

> Hear my voice when I call, LORD;
>   be merciful to me and answer me.
> My heart says of you, "Seek his face!"

Your face, LORD, I will seek.
Do not hide your face from me,
   do not turn your servant away in anger;
   you have been my helper.
Do not reject me or forsake me,
   God my Savior.
Though my father and mother forsake me,
   the LORD will receive me.
Teach me your way, LORD;
   lead me in a straight path
   because of my oppressors.
Do not turn me over to the desire of my foes,
   for false witnesses rise up against me,
   spouting malicious accusations.

I remain confident of this:
   I will see the goodness of the LORD
   in the land of the living.
Wait for the LORD;
   be strong and take heart
   and wait for the LORD. (Psalm 27:7–14)

Verses to Consider

Deuteronomy 31:8
Psalm 27

She Seems So Normal podcast

For more about body dysmorphia

Chapter 13

MARRIAGE

Sabotaging Narrative and My Husband's Toes

What soap operas do we insert in our mind space with our spouses or loved ones? When images from the past barge into our present, can we recognize the triggers and not react? Is it possible to create healthy boundaries after three decades of marriage? Yup.

 Narratives We Write About Others, Sometimes Without Their Permission

Deep inside and long ago, I penned a "sabotage narrative" about my beloved, truly doubting Christopher's intentions and feelings for me. In the cells of my being, my deeply held belief has been I'm unworthy of the man I married more than twenty-seven years ago. My jaded observations show he actually pities me, his pathetic wife, and is simply too loyal for divorce. When my therapist asked about him, I shared that I always was manipulative, choosing him specifically because he would never leave, even if I made him the most miserable man on earth. (In fact, I confidentially wondered if I was doing it while going through therapy.)

Gosh, when I read those pixels forming the words of

my thoughts, it seems so stupid. You know, sometimes seeing your thoughts on paper pulls them from darkness and places them in the fresh light of day.

Having been with Christopher for so long, I can now look back and see how he has proved his love for me over and over again. It's in the way he looks at me tenderly and smiles. When he walks by me, he reaches out to touch or hug me. He likes to make me laugh and is always joking to lighten my dark moods. He provides well for our family and loves our children dearly. He's an excellent father, church leader, entrepreneur, and businessman. He's a wonderful son. He is excellent and praiseworthy in all things. Except singing. (Don't ask him to sing.)

In short, Christopher has proven his trustworthiness throughout our marriage. He claims he fell in love with me the first time he saw me; we have the letter to his best friend to prove it. Actions speak louder than words, though. In August three decades ago after basic training at West Point Military Academy, I needed a mattress and bunk for my room. Christopher searched through the barracks to find both for me—his first act of great love. There have been so many others since then. I've only recently begun to realize why he did them.

I have often believed that people just put up with me, that once my usefulness was over, I would be kicked out the door. "Throwaway" is how I have described myself. Little did I know that this deep-seated belief was formed over years and years of lies implanted by the enemy in the most horrific ways.

So often, I wrongly assumed that I would somehow be fired, and I preempted that decision by leaving jobs because I didn't think I had anything else left to offer my employer or because I didn't think I had the staying power to have long-term relationships with people. I was the first to cut the rope and bail before anyone could hurt me because I was so afraid of their rejection. It's sabotage to think other people's thoughts for them, don't you think?

But people do it all the time.

We make ill-informed decisions because we think we know the full picture, but we don't. We come to decisions from a place of paranoia or fear or rejection, not from God's position of power, authority, or wisdom.

This is how I have lived for at least four decades. It's been absolute misery rejecting people before they could throw me away. My fear and paranoia were such a sneaky lie, such a subconscious thing until the Lord brought them into the light.

Can a Big Toe Really Make You Freak Out? (4.8.2020)

56

Christopher has a big toe joint that is swollen with arthritis from playing soccer most of his life. During the quarantine, he watched videos and became convinced he (we) could really help relieve some of the pressure by massaging and breaking up the bone spurs that had been plaguing him and making him so miserable.

He asked me repeatedly to help rub his foot and the joint that was giving him so much pain. I kept squirming out of this request. I could not bring myself to crack his foot bones and massage that gristly mass. It's not that I don't love my husband; it's that I don't love touching his feet.

One night, after brushing and flossing my teeth before bedtime, I gazed into the mirror and addressed my reflection. *Why can't I serve my husband in necessary and tangible ways with this foot thing?* I wavered, changed tact, and scoffed. *Seriously, who can blame me? Feet—ugh. Right?*

Why were my husband's feet making me feel so conflicted?

Then, an image came from out of nowhere. Swollen purple feet. Long and large, clearly belonging to a man, the yellowed toenails were gruesome. Feeling terrified and little, I recalled the enormous toenail clipper, the only kind able to cut the claws of an old man.

Losing composure as I write this, nervously fingering keystrokes on my computer to complete this picture, even now I shudder.

As I verbally processed this mental intrusion with Christopher, who was already snuggled in bed for the night, I explained it as simply as possible while, at the same time, pushing this image from my brain.

Circling like a mosquito you swat but can't kill, the memory persisted. Refusing to capitulate to another panic attack, I began trying every breathing technique to calm myself, working through my toolbox however I could to regain control.

I told Christopher that I needed to be held, and he gathered me into his arms. This stinking image convulsed my entire body defensively to repulse it, yet it was adamant to stay, refusing to be ignored. Desperately cocooning myself in a heavy down comforter, protecting my head and neck, peering up at Christopher's face, I hid, concealing any skin from sight.

Suddenly, full panic mode inside my chrysalis drew me underwater; I succumbed to PTSD's gripping fear. Grabbing my necklace, repeating my mantra, "I am near the cross, and Jesus is near me!" I panicked. Fight-or-flight parasympathetic response triggered, gasping to breathe, I began spinning out of control. Furiously falling tears blinded me; I couldn't see the room. I couldn't feel my husband. I lost it again.

After spending what felt like an eon in my head stuck in the past, I finally convinced myself to engage slower breathing with the knowledge that I had conquered attacks before. My mind snapped into a technique my therapist taught me ten days before: I began describing the details of our bedroom:

1. Three clerestory windows, the full moon shines.

2. The white paneled wall, our tea-stain colored linen headrest.

3. The cotton duvet softness covering my neck.

4. Christopher's slow, steady heartbeat thumping in my ear.

5. The warmth of his hand covering mine, the pressure between our fingers as I squeeze.

A desperate edge tinged my tone. "The memory can't hurt me, right?"

"Nope, it can't hurt you anymore," Christopher said.

"I'm in the present. With you, right?"

I began another new technique reciting birthdays, my Social Security number, and various math facts to deescalate myself. As a grown and married woman, at home I had nothing to fear anymore. Christ was with me. I had the power over what I did or didn't do. No one made me do things I didn't want to. I got to choose. This was going to end. Now.

And it did. A whole bevy of new power tools won the day once again.

Full-out panic attack time (from start to finish): 20 minutes.

Wow. That's progress.

Toes in Real Time, or, The Wins of Saying No and the Power of Being Honest

One night, I stretched on our bedroom floor as Christopher sat watching me from the bed, his legs overhanging. Glancing at the foot dangling near me, I noticed his toe was bleeding from where he had torn the nail too close to the quick. Eeewww.

My husband had major foot surgery late in 2020 and had been doing physical therapy for months. When he saw me looking at his foot, he began talking about the swollen knuckle, not realizing I was cringing because of the nail.

"Babe, look at it! My toe is feeling so much better. Look, I can move it up and down and there's more flexibility. I keep icing it. This stuff I'm doing is really working."

"Uh-huh. That's awesome, Sweetie. I'm glad it's getting better," I answered and continued to stretch, touching ankles and then toes. My hamstrings squealed they were so tight, and my lower back was sore from sitting at my computer too long writing.

"Just pull it out for me," he told me. "Go ahead! Grab that big toe and pull. Move it around and try to break up the junk."

Honestly, just looking at the red, swollen joint gave me a mini flashback that I had to push from my mind. No, no. no. NO.

"No, I'm sorry, I'm not going to do it," I said slowly,

"Wait, I'm not sorry. I am telling you what I need. I need to not do this. Truly," and the tears began to well up in my eyes again. He knew all about the trauma event; he was with me when it happened. It just didn't occur to him that it still lingered and affected me until I told him. Instead of doing what he asked and feeling ashamed, frustrated, and betrayed about doing it, I was finally using my voice to make choices that kept me from anger and resentment. This is called being honest and not making your husband guess why you're up in arms or being passive-aggressive toward him.

It felt good to be an adult. With another adult at my side.

When I think of the woman's description of her love in the Song of Songs, it reminds me of my Christopher:

> Listen! My beloved!
>   Look! Here he comes,
> leaping across the mountains,
>   bounding over the hills. (Song of Songs 2:8)

Verses to Consider

Ephesians 5:25–33
1 Peter 3:7

She Seems So Normal podcast

Chapter 14

HEALING AIN'T ALL CHAMPAGNE AND CAVIAR DREAMS

It's More Like Guns N' Roses:
The Exhausting Overwhelm

But he said to me, "My grace is sufficient for you, for my power is made perfect in weakness." Therefore I will boast all the more gladly about my weaknesses, so that Christ's power may rest on me.

—2 Corinthians 12:9

It's Too Much to Fix (2.28.2020)

41

As I pushed through therapy at breakneck speed, Michele told me she had rarely seen someone progress so quickly. It was a testament to my unfailing desire to obediently follow Christ, my readiness for change, God's perfect timing, and a breakthrough technique. I recognized the incredible leadership and support of medical professionals and cheering friends down the winding, ugly path to freedom.

As I relished breakthroughs into the past and knowledge of memories that haunted me for decades, another critical revelation hit: I was so broken and screwed up and felt I was beyond possible repair—a totaled vehicle destined for scrap metal.

The knowledge of family dynamics felt like a series of lies and cover-ups. The manipulation of memories into what seemed to be happy ones (when they really weren't) crashed through my emotional ceiling.

So.

Many.

Lies.

I always wondered why I could never get my ish together, always assuming there was something wrong with me. I was only beginning to discover the reasons for it all. At that point, it seemed easier to blame myself and box it up than confront it and see what it was.

Oh, Lord. Everything has changed. There is just too much work to do to get me well again. Constantly triggered, I felt more helpless and hopeless than ever before, and I couldn't do anything about it. Was ignorance bliss? Uh, yeah. How do you cure PTSD? Overcome moderate to major depression? Fix adjustment disorder with anxious mood? Or all the crazy listed in my medical file?

How could I get rid of flashbacks, panic attacks, depression, and anxiety? I was overwhelmed by how badly I had messed up my marriage, anxiety-parented my kids, and wasted so much time in life. This spiral had taken five decades to inexorably destroy those I loved the most in my life—my little family of Christopher, Julian, and Bella. As I realized the environment in my family of origin messed me up in too many ways, everything seemed so impossible and unredeemable.

Except . . . God brought to mind Joseph in Genesis 50, when all the lies were uncovered and his brothers realized the boy they had sold into slavery was now head over Egypt. After their father's funeral, the eleven siblings were terrified and worried that Joseph would execute them for their cruelty when he was younger. He reassured them: "You intended to harm me, but God intended it for good to accomplish what is now being done, the saving of many lives" (Genesis 50:20).

"But God intended it for good to accomplish . . . the saving of many lives." All this junk, the abuse and dysfunction the enemy thought would kill me wouldn't accomplish what he desired. I wasn't gonna let it. I was going to fight to get better, to come closer to Jesus in order to accomplish His purpose in the kingdom.

I'm praying this will help you and your life. So:

I will give my testimony of the goodness of God in the land of the living (Psalm 27:13).

I will throw off this yoke, the lies d'Evil whispered in my ear.

I will not be defeated.

Lord, may your will be accomplished in your servant. Help me persevere; give me strength and boldness to proclaim your grace and goodness to others who suffer like this. Heal me, Father, and help me when I cry out to you! I know you hear me and that you love your little children; you loved me so much that you sent your Son to show me the way. I trust in you completely.

This is all I know to do—pray and keep running. Throwing off what's holding me down, the entangling sin tripping me up, I reach toward the finish line, toward Jesus who's already endured and overcome! I refuse to get weary or lose heart. And if I do, you better come kick me in the butt if you're my friend!

> *Therefore, since we are surrounded by such a great cloud*
> *of witnesses, let us throw off everything that hinders*
> *and the sin that so easily entangles. And let us run with*
> *perseverance the race marked out for us, fixing our eyes*
> *on Jesus, the pioneer and perfecter of faith. For the joy*
> *set before him he endured the cross, scorning its shame,*
> *and sat down at the right hand of the throne of God.*
> *Consider him who endured such opposition from sinners,*
> *so that you will not grow weary and lose heart.*

—Hebrews 12:1–3

 He Sings Over Me

42

In the seventies, Waylon Jennings released "Amanda" on his album *The Ramblin' Man*, and the chorus repeats these lines: "Amanda, light of my life. Fate should have made you a gentleman's wife."[1]

More than four decades later, as summer sunshine filtered through an ivy trellis above red-and-white checkered tablecloths, the music playing on the patio was straight from a 1970s jukebox mix. I was triggered almost to the point of distraction. My heart was beating rapidly. I couldn't eat or concentrate. All I heard was the music.

Memories flooded my brain like a movie reel projected onto a cracked wall.

As preschool bus lights flashed, the driver asked me to sing for the kids. So, I sang my way to preschool, and at the end of the day, I sang all the way back home.

Little Me also remembers driving to jobsites in "Red Room" guy's big truck. A pioneer in preform concrete, he built prisons and hospitals all over the West. Singing to the radio at the top of my lungs, he smiled and encouraged me to learn those country-and-western songs by heart. His dog always sat between us.

At my preschool Head Start graduation, I sang the solo for my classmates and their families: "I've Been Working on the Railroad." Truly a proud moment I remember, it was a moment that made me want to be a singer when I grew up some day.

Celebrating that night by sipping Shirley Temples in the Highway Tavern and daintily eating tiny shrimps in cocktail sauce, I imagined being the queen of the world to have such success and eat such extravagant food. I fondly remember peeling back the aluminum top from the tall footed glasses and delightedly fishing out each delectable piece with the tiny appetizer fork.

My joy would be short-lived.

Lurking at the back of this tavern was a banquet hall turned storage room where they kept black stacked chairs and tables—the Red Room. I've known its location since the first PTSD event, but I have never trusted my own recall of the things that happened there.

My Solo Singing for School Stopped After Preschool Graduation

Later, I stood in smoky bars in front of countless jukeboxes singing for the people seated at high-top, fake red leather–covered bar stools that lined every carved-wood western tavern. Always dark and gloomy, those places had windows that were filthy from a hundred years of nicotine clouds, the once-cheery curtains stained with yellow tar. In every place each night, my sister and I sat helplessly tired and waiting to go home. The smoke and the drunks were the same too. Thrilled when I was beckoned to sing, one time I even stood onstage with Faron Young. For three minutes of adorable entertainment, I was the trained monkey, a flash in the pan until people got back to their drinks and their loud, slurred conversations. Sometimes my song and dance prompted "a round of drinks on me!" The crowd cheered, then laughed as my primary abuser cussed me out when the song was finished, and after my dismissal, the spotlight quickly fading, I shuffled back, dejected, to the dark booth in the corner.

The enemy tempts you to do what he asks and then makes a fool of you for doing it, doesn't he? I wonder if my abuser secretly enjoyed the masquerade of showing everyone his possession but was immediately jealous of their pleasure in my entertainment.

"Red Room" guy bought my breakfast, usually sweet milky tea with toast or hash browns. I guess to a child molester providing my room and board, I was worth the cost of tea and toast, but that doesn't seem to be fair barter for a child whose sexual abuse ended before she could spell *Czechoslovakia*.

After school, at a bar where yet another jukebox played the same country music and the stools were covered in the same red vinyl, I could order anything I wanted, usually an icy glass of Coke and chips or a candy bar. He gave me quarters galore for video games, and if it was a special day, he slipped me a dollar to go across the street to the general store for an ice cream or Hostess fruit pies.

More than forty years later, triggered by music from one barbecue birthday dinner, I realized this man valued me in junk food and video games.

Waylon's chorus and harmonies chased me, echoing through the ensuing hours, haunting me to the point of tears, and eventually leading to a panic attack the next day. The worst PTSD attacks seem to happen in my bedroom, and this one came while lying in bed face-to-face with Christopher. I confessed the anxiety and its root, this horrifying song and all it represented.

"You need a new song, Baby," my husband looked into my teary eyes with empathy. *Will I ever not be crying?* I wondered.

"I can't even think of a new song. This is on repeat every ten minutes in my head, and I can't get it out," I explained miserably. "Sing to me. Sing me something else. Please." I pleaded with him, knowing he didn't sing in front of others or feel comfortable doing this.

"OK. But it might sound bad."

"Chase the enemy away. I don't care!" I told him, desperate for relief.

He started slowly. It was a song from his father, one that he used to sing to Christopher and his siblings before bed each night. It was a song I knew so well; I sang it to my own babies.

If you'll be M-I-N-E mine, I'll be T-H-I-N-E thine.

And I will L-O-V-E love you all the T-I-M-E time.

You are the B-E-S-T best of all the R-E-S-T rest

and I will L-O-V-E love you all the T-I-M-E time!

"Sing it again."

And he did. As he sang it faster and faster (like his father did when my husband was a little boy), we began to laugh like he did as a little boy with his brothers and sister. The dark shadowed chorus of "Amanda" dissipated like smoke in the wind, chased away by a song from a father to his son, by the light of the love of a husband for his wife, by God to His people.

The Psalms often talk about how God in His grace gives us a new song to sing (see Psalms 33:3; 40:3; 98:1; 149:1). If there is a song stuck in your head that brings back dark memories, it's time for a new song.

Verses to Consider

Genesis 50:20

Psalm 27:12–13

Psalm 98:1–9

Zephaniah 3:14–20

She Seems So Normal podcast

PART 3

PLASTIC PRINCESS NO MORE

Embracing the "New Normal"
of Authentic Faith

Throwing rocks to break windows is easy. Cleaning glass slivers and shards, not so much. Piecing it back together? That's like a camel going through the eye of a needle. With man, it's impossible, but with God . . . well, God is the master of impossible (Matthew 19:23–26).

Parts 1 and 2 unpacked a lot of messy stuff, didn't they? I learned more about my life than I ever wanted to, and I imagine you might be feeling the same. Maybe you're wondering at this point, how does it end? An underlying theme embodying our Mackenzie family dynamics, professional lives, and ministries is, Do you want to be part of the problem or part of the solution?

Are there helpful solutions for people with trauma? Yes.

I've watched the Creator sweep my shattered, stained pieces into His own hands—shredding His own Son—to create new stained-glass windows from my broken parts, like those in grand old churches depicting Bible stories and parables. By day, the sun illuminates the details for those within as they worship, but by night, the light within shines through the story windows, marveling those outside their walls.

Here are a few lessons I've learned—or more accurately, continue learning—from leaving the plastic princess behind and embracing a better biblical journey with authentic faith.

Chapter 15

LESSON ONE: GOD SEES BEAUTY IN OUR BROKENNESS

God is near the brokenhearted. I'm not alone. I'm still standing.

If you take nothing else from this book, I pray these next words sink deep:

Despite everything you've done or that's been done to you, the Father has never, ever let go of you or left you. He's seen it all and is not disgusted with you or ashamed of you. God wants every line of promised Scripture to bring you healing and freedom. He brings darkness to light, so take every thought captive in obedience to Christ, demolish strongholds, and utilize the divine weapons of the Holy Spirit to move forward in faith.

- God hovers nearby in our suffering. God is near the brokenhearted and those who are downcast in spirit. He is slow to anger but abounding in love. He never leaves or forsakes you. The Wonderful Counselor doesn't leave us as orphans. Jesus prays for us. (Psalm 34:18; Hebrews 13:5; Isaiah 9:6; John 14:18; John 17:20–23)

- The right people are *for* you in/through suffering. Others have suffered, but some people dedicate their lifetimes to help. Paul's words resonate: "Who will rescue me from this body that is subject to death?" (Romans 7:24)

- Jesus embodies and identifies with suffering. It's the way of the cross and the door to the throne room to receive compassion. (Hebrews 4:14–16)

> *What has been will be again, what has been done*
> *will be done again; there is nothing new under the*
> *sun. Is there anything of which one can say, "Look!*
> *This is something new"? It was here already,*
> *long ago; it was here before our time.*
> —Ecclesiastes 1:9–10

♕ What's Beautiful to God?

44

Who is *not* affected by suffering? No one. And God sees our pain.

During invitation time at church, the wooden steps show the tears of everyone who had poured out their suffering before the Lord and begged for His mercy and blessing, His wisdom and guidance. My heart aches from the suffering of God's people—whether it was due to the consequences of their own sinful actions, because someone hurt them, or because of the sin from a fallen world.

We have been wounded. All of us.

I've personally come to know the Great Physician, God Almighty, in the person of Jesus Christ, that "the punishment that brought us peace was on him, and by his wounds we are healed" (Isaiah 53:5), that He was "a man of suffering, and familiar with pain" who "took up our pain and bore our suffering" (vv. 3 and 4). "Yet it was the LORD's will to crush him and cause him to suffer" (v. 10), but "he bore the sin of many, and made intercession for the transgressors" (v. 12).

I am the transgressor.

You are the transgressor.

We are *all* transgressors.

If we don't know what Jesus has done, our wounds heal funny, or not at all. We get contorted spiritually and emotionally. We get deformed instead of re-formed, like the marred clay in the hands of the potter in Jeremiah (Jeremiah 18:4).

Grace was birthed through pain and suffering. Christ after the passion and crucifixion was unrecognizable (Isaiah 52:14), marred by the sin of the world.

We are all marred by the sin of the world. It may have been today or last week or a long time ago when we were little. There are times that even as a Christian I have become unrecognizable. The sin upon me was so great—from past oppression, from the sin of others, from my own sin, from not believing that God is who He says He is or who I am in Him.

The enemy tried carving the word *UNHOLY* all over me, but Christ's blood sank deep into the crevices left by those lies, much like the liquid gold holding together broken pieces of Japanese *kintsugi* masterpieces, drowning them completely in perfect love through His suffering at Calvary. When we become unrecognizable, we share that with Jesus Christ, but He already suffered so that we would have a way out of our pain. We may get lost, but we can be found in Him. His suffering birthed His grace, His unmerited favor upon us.

Suffering produces pain, but we don't like pain. Pain sharpens senses, heightening awareness. Little did I realize that I would be going through major trials of my own, that God would be testing me heavily in this season. Foolishly, I thought I would view this process in the third person until God literally brought this teaching home to my doorstep.

What is beautiful to God? What is good to God? His idea of beauty and goodness is not how we would define it if it were left up to us. When I think of what is "good" for myself, for my family, or for others, it does not necessarily line up with what God has for me. Sometimes the road is one of suffering, but if this is what it takes for me to grow up in Christ and depend on Him, to believe in His goodness and love in a more personal and intimate way, so be it!

This is where the rubber meets the road in our faith. All the Bible study, prayer, fasting, worshipping, tears, and the years when He used teachers, pastors, mentors, and the Holy Spirit helped me become a "worker who does not need to be ashamed and who correctly handles the word of truth" (2 Timothy 2:15).

We are all broken by sin. But God loves broken people. And that's a good thing *because broken people are all He has*. When we don't understand that He loves us in spite of our brokenness, we have to fight through our feelings for the identity that is already ours in Jesus. Our default is listening to d'Evil's voice denying our beauty. But God's Word is true.

So, we fight. I call this the "beautiful fight." Paul writes about this victorious battle in Ephesians 6.

👑 What Is the Beautiful Fight?

45   The beautiful fight means we fight to die to ourselves daily and take up the cross of Jesus Christ.

The beautiful fight means we fight for our marriages to look like God has modeled them in His Word.

The beautiful fight means we fight for our children by the grace and strength of Jesus Christ. We wage this one constantly on our knees when they are teenagers.

The beautiful fight means we fight to maintain the purity of our minds and our bodies, to not seek the affections or attentions or affirmations of men but trust in the Lord to appoint and anoint the godly Christian men we will, God willing, one day marry.

The beautiful fight means we fight our addictions and the strongholds of our sin in the power of the Holy Spirit, knowing that by the blood of Jesus Christ, the power of sin and death and our past is broken. There is now no condemnation in Christ! We are set free!

The beautiful fight means we fight illness or disease, or watch our loved ones do it, and give Christ the glory whatever the outcome.

The beautiful fight means we fight to submit to one another out of reverence for Christ, to live in honor and to consider others' needs more than our own, to be in unity with the Holy Spirit as we serve this beautiful church.

The beautiful fight means we fight in that hospital room to keep up the faith, to believe that God is good even when our circumstances are screaming for us to believe He is not.

The beautiful fight means we fight to make time to serve lost people through various ministry opportunities, showing them how much God loves them by taking time to listen, answer their questions, and love them all the way to the throne of Jesus.

The beautiful fight means we fight the ideals of this world and remember that the kingdom of God is what's real in this life.

The beautiful fight means we fight to be constantly aligned with the Holy Spirit inside our hearts when the enemy threatens to unbalance the world around us through political, social, or racial divisions, pandemics and mental health diseases, power-hungry and paranoid world leaders, environmental disasters, or plain apathy to the plight of our neighbors and fellow man.

The beautiful fight means we fight to make disciples of Jesus Christ and take ground for the kingdom of God and, in so doing, hasten Christ's coming.

The beautiful fight means we fight our fear of the unknown by emerging from our comfort zones to serve the Lord on mission trips in our cities, across our nation, and all over the earth.

The beautiful fight means we fight to offer a sacrifice of praise and to worship God—the Creator of the universe—even when we don't feel like it.

The beautiful fight means we fight to trust God and all His promises, to stand on the truth of the Scriptures, even in the face of circumstances that seem overwhelmingly unfair, unkind, and unredeemable. The beautiful fight means enduring suffering beautifully.

Here's a powerful spiritual warfare prayer from the book *The Adversary*:

> I thank You for these battles and all that You are
> seeking to accomplish in Your wisdom and design

for my life. I accept the battle and rejoice in Your purpose. I willingly accept and desire to profit from all of Your purpose in letting Satan's kingdom get at me. I reject all of Satan's purpose. Through the victory of my Lord and Savior I stand resolute and strong upon the certainty of my victory. In confidence I look to You, Lord Jesus Christ. When your purpose for this trial is fulfilled, I know that it shall fade into the dimness of forgotten battles and a defeated enemy. Though the precious name of the Lord Jesus Christ, it shall be so. Amen.[1]

How to Fight the Beautiful Fight

1. The Beautiful Fight Waged on Your Knees:
   - Soldiers regularly radio commanders to receive updated instructions. We pray, read the Bible, and seek godly counsel to determine God's instructions to us.
   - Whether you stand or kneel, *don't forget where He sits*! Hebrews 12:2 (NIV84) says: "Let us fix our eyes on Jesus, the author and perfecter of our faith, who for the joy set before him endured the cross, scorning its shame and sat down at the right hand of the throne of God."
   - Remain under the umbrella of God's protection during the consequences of sin and suffering. Whatever the circumstance, just remain under.
   - In God's economy, tears are held as prayer, so when something is unspeakably overwhelming for us, God honors groans of the Spirit.

2. The Beautiful Fight Waged Shoulder to Shoulder:

- Soldiers never disconnect from their squad, so why would we ever give up meeting together, having accountability and fellowship? Continuing connection and fellowship with the body of believers spurs us on through encouragement.

- Are we willing to be accountable? You don't have to bare your soul to everyone (in fact, you shouldn't), but you do need a band of believers around you. Set the plastic aside in these transparent, trustworthy circles, and let the light of the gospel expose your true beauty—flaws, flab, fears, and all.

- Are you willing to disciple others? Military soldiers rarely move down in rank, only up, training others and becoming mentors as they ascend and having mentors who teach them their next job. We need people to disciple and people who disciple us. Who's been around awhile or new to the faith? Those might be your people.

3. The Beautiful Fight Waged Head to Toe:

- Like battlefield soldiers, we live in life-and-death situations. Faith and suffering are not a game. People's lives are at stake—including yours. Are you all in or not?

- Let's be bold and practice the greatest commandment mentioned in four different books of the Bible, Old Testament and New, and three times by Jesus: Love the Lord your God with all your heart, mind, soul, and strength.[2] This head-to-toe command covers our affections, actions, beliefs, and thoughts so we can love our neighbors better.

- Do we have skin in the game? Following Christ is a full-time profession, not a side gig, and it's 100 percent not a part-time stint.
- Take a single step closer to up your ante and amp up your game.

Our goal is Christ. With our last exhale on earth, there should be nothing left *in us* or *of us* on the glorious day we enter the throne room!

Verses to Consider

Isaiah 53
John 17:20–23
Romans 8:26
Ephesians 6
Colossians 3:13–14
Hebrews 4:14–16
Hebrews 10:24–25

She Seems So Normal podcast

Chapter 16

♔ LESSON TWO: AVOID ISOLATION
—IT'S DARK AND DANGEROUS

32

Isolation used to be one of my favorite coping strategies. A "shut down, shut out" kinda girl, any time people got too close, I shut them down, shut them out, and walked away satisfied that I controlled the terms of my emotional intimacy and relationships. In challenging times at school, work, or church or with neighbors, friends, or family members, my play often became not calling or returning texts, suddenly dropping out of social events and, in general, disappearing. "Ghosting" has become a thing now, but I've been doing it forever. Being groomed and programmed for abuse taught me well. When *no* is ignored, traumatized people have other ways to deal with pain. As a child, the "There's no going for help—no one is going to rescue me" belief of learned powerlessness (remember the baby elephant?) and the secrecy requirements common with abuse killed any hope of changing my interactions with the world. Isolation slowly killed my soul.

The Enemy Knows Isolation Is One of the Most Powerful Tools in His Arsenal

Don't confuse solitude with isolation. Time alone with God is good. Richard Foster in *Celebration of Discipline* and other experts encourage the spiritual discipline of solitude. Throughout the Gospels, praying and seeking His Father's will, Jesus was drawn to wide-open wastelands, lonely mountaintops, and hillside gardens. Ahead of vital turning points in His public ministry, Jesus was alone and praying—through His temptation in the desert, before calling His disciples, and preceding His walk on the waters of Galilee. After a busy day of ministry teaching and healing the sick and possessed in Capernaum, Jesus wandered off again: "Very early in the morning, while it was still dark, Jesus got up, left the house and went off to a solitary place, where he prayed" (Mark 1:35).

However, these times of solitude were the exception and not the rule. At the transfiguration, Peter, James, and John accompanied Jesus. When He prayed in Gethsemane's garden to confirm God's will, He brought the same three again. Throughout most of His ministry, Jesus walked closely with the disciples.

There's a difference between quietly communing with the Father on a hilltop and sharing communion with the enemy in our heads. One spiritually blesses and builds us up; the other spiritually bludgeons and bleeds us dry.

Peter wrote this to Christians undergoing persecution for their faith in Asia Minor (present-day western

Turkey): "Be alert and of sober mind. Your enemy the devil prowls around like a roaring lion looking for someone to devour" (1 Peter 5:8).

While that's the third time in that letter Peter warned believers to be alert and self-controlled, it was his first time elaborating on the source of their persecution by providing a very real and understandable word picture. Our choice to remain in solitary, lonely places allows the enemy access to our souls, like a single lion's ambush, which silently surprises, suffocates, then kills its prey.

Wanna know what happened to fluffy felines when judges, kings, prophets, and evangelizers encountered them in the past? They were either ripped apart with bare hands, killed in pits on snowy days, or muzzled by the power of God. (Think Samson, David, Benaiah, Daniel, and Paul in 2 Timothy 4:17.)

Isolation makes us forget our resources and our identity, and we so easily forget, don't we? Without the Holy Spirit's power, we become powerless against lion schemes. If we don't know our identity in Christ or trust God's omnipotent power and infinite goodness, the enemy can trick us into dangerous isolation, eviscerating us slowly, devouring mouthful after toothy mouthful.

Able to twist even the best-intentioned godly practices like solitude into knots of spiritual isolation, d'Evil ties ribbons laced with deceitful half-truths and shame into contorted constructs of demonic control. He almost succeeded with me.

👑 Plastic-Princess Transparency Deconstruction
33 Moment #2—Blog Post from The Church Girl Writes: Writing Through Suicidal Thoughts

Being extremely transparent with you in this post. Writing and sharing this piece helped pull me out of this dark time.

Some days it's hard to put on a pretty face.

Tears welling in my eyes make my mascara goopy instead of crisp and thick as sloppy smears pool then roll down my cheeks. *Gotta pull it together, Princess*, a voice speaks at the mirror's reflection of me. *You have things to do.*

Can I summon the will to live right now? Sometimes there are days when all I can say is "I'm sorry."

Désolé. (Translation: inconsolably sad, sorry.)

Last week, with no explanation, I asked my husband to take every medicine I was prescribed after my last bout with depression, anxiety, and suicide two years ago and dispose of them at the health department. I told him we didn't need these in the house anymore.

So tired of feeling, so tired of therapy—so tired of so many things—but mostly, I am SO tired of me. In fact, Christopher knows nothing about my fantasies of swallowing all the pills at once and has no idea that in the last ten days, I considered leaving to be with Jesus more times than I'd like to admit.

Désolé. (Translation: desolate, afraid.)

Hopelessness rises, blotting out my spirit. *I am such a cowardly Christian.* Shouldn't I have a heart more valiant, a faith more bold, and a more enduring hope than what I can muster right now? The darkness expands today as the flicker of light shrinks.

Soul weariness. I'm coated in a sheen of detachment and have no energy to fight. Every attempt to soak in Scripture shows my despairing soul bound and tethered to the weight pulling me deep into the earth.

Does Jesus work for people like me in real life?

Eternal salvation I don't doubt; I'm saved for eternity in heaven because of the blood, cross, and resurrection. However, right now, I'm not sure if I want to take time to sort through the "mess of me" because there's too much to heal, too much to figure out, and too much visceral pain breaking my life. Listening to a sermon in church, I wondered if there is a trauma survivor's translation of the Bible, wondered if preaching pastors could possibly understand the depths and complicated nature of mental illness of the people in their pews. These thoughts pound in between the first and last sets as I lead praise and worship onstage.

Désolé. (Translation: contrite, penitent.)

Put on the face and get out there, Princess!

Lord, why am I such a fraud? Who am I to sing and praise you onstage while these thoughts plague me in the seats? Is this a sacrifice of praise to give thanks even while I don't feel like it? Silently confessing my weakness, unbelief, and lack of trust in the God who has been by my side and never left me, I pray for true godly repentance, but what I really want and need is forgiveness and absolution.

And yet . . . Jesus knows all this. He still lets me sit in it with Him. Wait, no, He's sitting with me because He's not a pushy savior, but a kind and gentle one (Matthew 11:28–30). Not a single demand to just "figure it out" or a plea for me to "look on the bright side"—things the well-meaning say because they've never traipsed across this desperate wasteland. Many of us walking waist-high through the swirling sands don't want to even consider, let alone see, tomorrow.

With a reassuring hand on His child's shoulder, the Father sits ready to listen as the Holy Spirit hovers quietly nearby as a forcefield keeping the enemy at bay. Gratitude, like butterfly's wings, brushes my heart for this reprieve.

Father, forgive me. What do I do now? I murmur. I don't want to worry anyone; I'm not to a point where I'm unsafe.

Faces come to mind, so I reach out to these prayer partners. Ashamed of my weakness, the words still tumble through my fingers onto the keyboard. "Would you mind praying for me? I'm in dark places trying to break the surface."

Immediately the enemy pounces: *What must it look like for a supposedly mature Christian woman to be on the edge like this? "She of little faith,"* he hisses.

Before I can answer, a text interrupts the demonic conversation before it begins.

My girlfriend knows I have been working to memorize part of Psalm 91, the Warrior's Poem, so she sends it:

If you make the LORD your refuge,
   if you make the Most High your shelter,
no evil will conquer you;
   no plague will come near your home.
For he will order his angels
   to protect you wherever you go.
They will hold you up with their hands
   so you won't even hurt your foot on a stone.
You will trample upon lions and cobras,
   you will crush fierce lions and serpents
   under your feet! (vv. 9–13 NLT)

Another text quickly follows, reminding me of Peter on the water with Jesus in the storm. Knowing both walking-on-water moments and ones where we are sinking, she asks for the shelter of security under the comfort of God's wings, requesting God grant me the courage of Joshua and Caleb in the land of their enemies, and that I remember God is greater than any dark forces that come.

So, I praise God for the trials, praise Him for the pain because I know He identifies with me through it all. He's the One who rescues me. Hiding in the palms of His capable hands, I'm covered in love, acceptance, and grace. Not fear. Not shame. In this safe place, my name is inscribed forever. What God's hand holds He never loses.

Today, I place my confidence in that truth. It's enough.

Francine Rivers, my wise mentor at the time, commented on the post:

You are in good company, Leigh. As you shared—David struggled and poured out his heart through the Psalms. I can hear your heart cry and am praying for you. What a loving God we have, for we know He is right there with us every minute. I am thankful you are sharing this journey because there are so many around us who are going through similar trials. When we know, we can come alongside and hold a hand, give a hug, just be present as we sit in loving silence.[1]

Wondering how to help someone who struggles? Do what Francine said. Come alongside, hold a hand, give a hug, just be present, and sit in loving silence. You'll never know the power of a single encouraging text, meaningful hug, or word aptly spoken . . . until you find it saved someone's life.

> *Take no part in the unfruitful works of darkness, but instead expose them. For it is shameful even to speak of the things that they do in secret. But when anything is exposed by the light, it becomes visible, for anything that becomes visible is light. Therefore it says,*
> *"Awake, O sleeper,*
> *and arise from the dead,*
> *and Christ will shine on you."*
>
> —Ephesians 5:11–14 ESV

Three Ways Satan Tries to Isolate Us

50

Schemes of the devil aren't anything new, so being alert and aware of a few of his common methods might help us stand in victory a little more and get devoured a little less.

Lies and Temptation. d'Evil is the father of lies. First John tells us to test the spirits. Not everything is riddled in worms and decay when the enemy begins—he makes temptation look *tempting*. Because it looks good, it seems to fill a deep, even godly longing/need. The enemy will keep you busy performing as a plastic Christian to keep you from fulfilling God's best. For a while, he convinced me it was easier to be a champion at church or work than to serve my first, highest ministry priority, my own family, and to strive to become a better wife/ mom at home.

Clever Negotiation. The serpent hissed, "Did God really say?" And he still does. The enemy tempts us to doubt God's goodness, mercy, and greatness. The best trial lawyers who win the most cases are often ones most familiar with the law. Jesus stops the devil's temptations in the desert with His robust familiarity with Scripture. How well do we know it? "All Scripture is God-breathed and is useful for teaching, rebuking, correcting and training in righteousness, so that the servant of God may be thoroughly equipped for every good work" (2 Timothy 3:16–17).

Shame Remuneration. "Oops, I did it again," to quote Britney Spears. Fool me once shame on you; fool me twice, shame on me, right? How many times will we go back to our folly, like a dog to its vomit (2 Peter 2:22)? Don't worry, the enemy will be sure to list every sinful offense so we're sure to remember them. It's hard to see through the bars of our shame cages when we're scared God can't or won't redeem our sin/circumstances. The enemy particularly enjoys emphasizing God's wrath and justice while minimizing His grace, mercy, and forgiveness through the blood of Jesus.

Turning Isolation to "I Solution"

While I still isolate at times, these days, I'm a lot quicker at asking for help. How did I do it?

By finding better solutions. I sought professional therapy, established deep, relational spiritual mentorships, created a prayer warrior tribe, and curated gratitude for my family, friends, community, and church.

Therapy helped me understand my past; I'm learning to love and be kind to myself. My spiritual mentors kept pointing me back to God's goodness and truth, encouraging me to keep going even when things seemed too hard. Cheering me daily, my accountability partners and friends offered support and the tools missing from my "daily life skills" box.

#gamechangers

So, what's my plan? Avoid isolation, cuz it's a dark and dangerous place.

Resist him, standing firm in the faith, because you know that the family of believers throughout the world is undergoing the same kind of sufferings.

And the God of all grace, who called you to his eternal glory in Christ, after you have suffered a little while, will himself restore you and make you strong, firm and steadfast. To him be the power for ever and ever. Amen.

—1 Peter 5:9–11

Verses to Consider

Genesis 3
1 Chronicles 11:22
2 Timothy 3:16–17
2 Timothy 4:17

She Seems So Normal podcast

For more about anxiety

Chapter 17

LESSON THREE: TOOLS OF THE TRAUMA TRADE—GOD IS ENOUGH/GOD'S TOOLBOX

A three-year-old's coping methods are primitive for fixing major trauma, like using a child's Fisher Price toolbox to fix a burst pipe. My go-to bright primary-color plastic hammer, screwdriver, and wrench were acting out, dissociating, and denial.

As a formerly compliant child, my "acting out" looked like defiance and manifested as extreme temper tantrums and breaking things. In my teenage years, it ramped up to emotional manipulation, eating disorders, and sexual promiscuity. You or your loved ones may act out by cutting, hurting animals, fighting, chemical/sexual/emotional addictions, or an entire host of other antisocial behaviors.

During incomprehensible, unresolvable childhood experiences, I began dissociating as my conscious mind left to go elsewhere for protection. Since I had run out of strategies to resolve or end the abuse, my spirit retreated to fantasy worlds spun in my mind through the books I read, or my senses focused on something tangible. Hyper-focusing in great singular detail became detailed hyper-analysis of, say, fabric wallpaper, ceiling tile patterns, car dashboards, stale cigarette smells, or carpet fiber texture in different times and places. Either way, I "won" because I didn't have to pay attention to what was happening to my body.

Years ago on a mission trip, long before learning anything of my own story, I spoke with a stunning young woman on a dusty fútbol field in the favelas of Rio de Janeiro, Brazil. A former child prostitute, she shared how she helped others endure years of trafficking and explained in Portuguese, "Sua mente leva você para outro lugar." *Your mind carries you elsewhere to another place.* That's about right.

After years of helping others who experienced systematic abuse (like incest) or sexual assault, I wondered about possible spiritual reasons for blocking trauma recall. Sitting across from one woman describing cult abuse, I caught a glimpse of Jesus putting His hands on either side of her head, saying, "Don't look anywhere else except me. Don't bother with what's happening to your body right now, concentrate on me. I have you." Could our gracious Savior shield us from unimaginable terror using dissociation? I wouldn't doubt it; He's got some pretty powerful tools.

Denial shuts down any acceptance, belief, or recognition that something bad is happening. Denial can stem from fear or memory repression. Many traumatized people lose large chunks of memory. That's also why people interviewed after physical battery, rape, sexual assaults, or other major trauma might not recall specific details later. Many survivors spend every moment trying to forget. Witnessing congressmen and lawyers running victims through the wringer to testify publicly simply because the court demands more details to satisfy juries and Senate panels and convict predators with multiple counts or accusations frustrates and disheartens those standing in the shadows wondering whether they'll recall enough to report their own experiences.

While I'm hesitant to label my primitive, Fisher Price–level coping mechanisms as "bad" because they kept me alive and equipped me to survive, over the years I developed more sophisticated behaviors than the public meltdowns from when I was six by observing and copying how others managed stress and anxiety, which helped me into adulthood. However, many of my newly cultivated skills weren't more positive or helpful than Fisher Price but maddeningly self-destructive, self-defeating, and more like endless cycles of sabotage. Nothing I did solved the problem.

But it's funny. When you come to the point that you realize *all* you have is Jesus, you find He is enough. And His toolbox has what we need.

Grown-Up Toolboxes (Authentic Faith: God Is Enough)

Ever been wide awake or awakened from sleep to find yourself terrified, soaking in sweat, with your pulse rate skyrocketing? Panic attacks stink, huh?

See, I used to melt down and

- fret for hours (my husband called this "piddling" before we knew what it was),

- emotionally vomit self-talk,
- have conversations with people who weren't there,
- verbally put myself down,
- physically hit myself to see if I still felt anything,
- cry and become paralyzed OR become so provoked and upset I yelled and screamed for little or no reason,
- pick at scabs, pimples, or hangnails until they bled,
- clean obsessively (though not productively),
- avoid people OR throw myself at them for distraction,
- numb myself with alcohol,
- exercise obsessively,
- eat everything and purge OR, conversely, eat nothing and starve,
- contemplate abandoning ship and disappearing like a runaway,
- and occasionally, fantasize about ways to not live.

For those who are struggling, coping strategies can be as individual as fingerprints. Now that I understand my traumatized brain wiring, I know those primitive coping mechanisms, which worked before, aren't a good option because I've been given *way* more effective and less self-destructive power tools to love myself and those around me.

When I find myself in the middle of big emotions or anxiety, it's difficult to think rationally. A written list helps provide a map for managing. You're welcome to borrow any of the ideas in the next section.

Anxiety

Did you know anxiety can include generalized anxiety disorder (GAD), panic attacks, social anxiety, and PTSD? According to the international nonprofit organization Anxiety and Depression Association of America, anxiety disorders are the most common form of mental health problems, affecting more than forty million adults in America, or one in five people.[1] Many are undiagnosed or not getting help because of the associated stigma or shame, especially inside the church. Chances are, you or someone you know suffers from anxiety. According to Tim Newman, "Anxiety is only a problem when it extends beyond logical worry in an unreasonable, unwarranted, uncontrollable way. Situations that should elicit no negative emotions all of a sudden seem life-threatening or crushingly embarrassing."[2]

Move into Better Tools

This is a laundry list, but what I've found works best is the Threefold Basic B Combo: Breath, Brain, Blessing

BREATH

Slow Breathing. Here's a tasty idea: imagine an enormous birthday cupcake. The candle flame quivers atop thick buttercream icing. Holding your cupcake in front of you, blow out the candle, feeling your breath across your palm. Do this ten times (or however many you can do before you pass out). Also, look up alternate nostril breathing techniques, meditative breathing apps, or ambient music online (such as in the apps Calm or Abide) to diffuse hyperventilation.

Speak Your Truth. Identify emotions or potential events causing anxiety and speak intention into existence. Breathe and speak: "I'm feeling _____ but I have power to do something about it."

Share Your State of the Union. If heads of state give one, why not you? Call or text trusted godly friends when you're struggling. Ask them to pray or speak aloud God's loving peace over you. Write the names of key lifeline people so when you need them, they're in front of you. In the middle of anxiety attacks, I couldn't recall a single person's name for help.

BRAIN/BODY

Step Away from the Caffeine. Amped and anxious? Step off the stimulants inflaming your parasympathetic nervous system and opt for gulping cool glasses of water or sipping herbal tea as a practical physical way to calm your nerves.

Scent and Sniff. My EMDR therapist provided a citrus blend to shock my senses to reality. Peppermint and fir worked well too.

See the Room. Describing the physical room brings your brain into the present. (Example: count ceiling tiles.) My therapist used this method with me several times during PTSD events to shift my brain from the imagery and emotion of past trauma back into real-time, fact-based thinking in the frontal cortex.

Simple Math. Using factual recall works wonders during attacks. Simple math facts (2 + 2 = ?, 4 + 4 = ?) shifts the brain into critical thinking mode. Count backward from one hundred by sevens. List children, pets, schoolteachers, or second-grade soccer teammates. State birthdates, wedding anniversaries, the GDP of Ethiopia, Social Security numbers,[3] or any listable facts. This easy, incredible method tricks the brain back into rational thinking and out of parasympathetic fight/flight/freak mode.

Scribe. Journal emotions, thoughts, or beliefs. Take thoughts captive; make 'em obedient to Christ. Capture hurricane swirls with ink nails on wood pulp. Analyzing irrational thoughts by pinning them to pixels or paper destroys their power by offering clarity and understanding.

Say What? "This one or that?" A high school dean worked a miracle before my eyes after an angry student marched in and cussed up a storm. Smiling and pointing, she asked where the girl wanted to sit. The miraculous power of simple choice dulled the teenager's daggers down to butter knives. Ask yourself to choose: *This or that?*

Shake Your Worship Booty. King David sang, danced, and shook his body. Crank the music and dance with your roomies! Walk or run with worship tunes. Expending stress energy moves me through emotions faster.[4]

Snuggle Down. Weighted blankets and hugs from safe people are my happiness. I've "cocooned" during panic attacks, protecting the back of my neck, ears, and head along with intimate body parts. I'm a physical touch kinda gal. If you're this way, too, you can also pet your dog or handle your hamster. No judgment here . . . you do you, Boo.

Surrender. You keep thinking *I can get ahead of this*, but many times you can't because of chemicals coursing through the brain. There is no shame using medicine when you need it to control anxiety or depression.

BLESSING

Slip On Spiritual Armor. Ephesians 6. Read it and literally go through the motions.

Scripture Speaks. God's truth works wonders. Refer to the verses provided at the end of each chapter in this book. Ask friends and pastors for favorites. Topically search the YouVersion app or Bible concordances. Post verses in your journal or on note cards, and scatter 'em like confetti in the car, on your mirror, at work— all over! Create/borrow beautiful graphics, add them as wallpaper on your phone, and share them on social media. Reading Jesus's words aloud when the enemy comes knocking on the door of my mind, soul, and heart makes d'Evil tremble.

Seize a Scriptural Mantra. Combined with a physical grounding touch piece like a cross, necklace, or stuffed animal, the mantra "I am near the cross and Jesus is near me" shifted me from PTSD to peace.

ADDITIONAL SELF-CARE IDEAS

Stick It in a Box. Once, after a particularly disturbing PTSD event at the end of an EMDR session, there wasn't time for unraveling a memory, so we boxed it up to keep until the next session. My wild imagination conjured a stark-white box wrapped in blue satin-silk bows. As you know, I've subconsciously boxed memories before, but that was my first time intentionally, productively shelving one.

Siesta. Care for yourself when it's finished. Quietly

meditate (or briefly hide in your closet from your kids). Catch some zzz's. Rest can make all the difference in finishing your day strong.

So, whatcha gonna use for your anxiety/panic attack? Create and write your own list. Steal some of mine. Prepare and strategize before the attack takes you out of the game. Will you follow it perfectly the first time? Doubtful, but with more practice comes progress, and we can acquire a practical discipline of mental health mastery over time.

The point of this chapter is to refocus your attention and turn your mind to this truth: God. Is. Enough. Jesus. Is. Enough. The Spirit in me. Is. Enough. Retrain your mind to gaze upon God and only glance on your past.

God's Limitless Toolbox

We all have our own toolboxes, but God's tools are limitless. The book of Genesis reveals He's got hard sciences like physics, genetics, astronomy, and biology in His back pocket. He nails complicated interpersonal human relationships until the Bible ends in Revelation 22. The Exodus signs and wonders of bloody rivers and boils, insects, and amphibians released more than a million slaves at once. A meteorological maven, He wiped the slate of wickedness with a world full of water and saved faithful Noah. On Sodom He sent fire, brimstone, and giant hailstones as spiritual exclamation points. The Lord has always included mankind in His toolbox, defeating marauding armies through praying prophets, fleece-testing judges, shepherd boys, and even a fierce woman named Jael, who served a platter of warm milk, a hammer, and a tent peg.

A chip off the Father's block, Jesus rebuked storms

and seas, but He also healed the lame, blind, and bleeding along with the distressed, diseased, and demonic, all with the touch of His hand or a word from His mouth. The Son holds the keys to victory in heaven, on earth, or any realm of the universe.

You might think, *That's all past*, but I believe God's mightiest implement for us today hovers over the waters "in the beginning" and fills Yahweh's followers with miraculous courage, wisdom, and strength through the ages, including those who patiently scribed Scripture on pen-scratched parchment with God-breathed truth that is as vitally relevant now as it was when ink stained the papyrus then.

The Spirit of God still moves, defeating tendrils of darkness with whispers of light, calling forth life from death. While I may offer a few good trauma tools, God provides the greatest ones because RESURRECTION is one of Holy Spirit's divine specialties.

Verses to Consider

Genesis 1–3	John 16:33
Psalm 4:8	1 Corinthians 2:16
Isaiah 12:2	Ephesians 6
Isaiah 26:3	Philippians 4:9

She Seems So Normal podcast

For more about EFT tapping

Chapter 18

LESSON FOUR: BEING A PLASTIC PRINCESS IS PAINFUL (AND HURTS EVERYONE)

Looking like you've got it together hurts everyone. It's hard to keep up a facade when you know it's fake. From recent news reports, it seems the higher one's religious or secular leadership status and breadth of influence, the more a facade is used to avoid accountability and keep secrets. No wonder we're shocked when go-to faves fall from grace; everyone's damaged by the aftermath.

Suicide Is off the Table—No Christmas Card 35, 36 for YOU

As the pandemic began, I was awakened in the middle of the night during the quarantine by Julian gaming online with his friends, and honestly, I lost my ish. Old me was back again, unrested and unhinged from late bedtimes the past few nights.

What do you suppose I did? If you said, "You got into a full-blown argument with your beloved, graduated, responsible teenage son," you are correct.

Have you ever seen anyone throw gasoline on a small flame? KaBOOM. That was me, tired and startled, and all it took was one late-night, smart-aleck comment to set the bonfire raging.

After a bit, I knew I had to stop, but once an argument has begun, it's like putting out a Chicago warehouse fire: firefighters douse structures with water, waiting until fuel and oxygen run out and the flames are extinguished.

Why couldn't I stop once I had started? That stupid parasympathetic reaction still programmed my brain, flooding cortisol stress hormones into my receptors. This time it was not a flight or freak—it was a raging fight for fifteen minutes that needed to stop.

Amped up yet panicking in this verbal conflagration, knowing I couldn't self-soothe easily, I sprinted down the darkened hall at 3:00 a.m. into the bathroom.

What do you suppose my concerned, argumentative, but well-meaning son did? He wanted to finish the fight. (#LoveYourStrongWilledChild) He followed me into the bathroom, rightly exclaiming how unfair and plain rude I was. I howled for him to leave me alone. Nice? No.

Anxiety level: 100 percent.

"Seriously, LEAVE. ME. ALONE!" I yelled. Propped up on his elbow in bed, a bleary-eyed Christopher rubbed his face.

Exhausted father directed frustrated son: "Julian, just go."

"What if she hurts herself? Then I'm responsible for her," he said tearfully.

Stop. Right. There.

Imagine this weight and worry for a child. He had reason for concern since long ago self-harm had been an option for me. I had a better toolbox now, but that wasn't clear to Julian, who would shoulder the guilt if he thought he was to blame. My child should not have that kind of burden.

Two anxious hours working through coping mechanisms (see the list in chapter 17) and reassuring self-talk calmed the triggers of being startled awake, hearing heavy footsteps in hallways, and getting into heated arguments. I finally was able to sleep.

We talked the next day. Sitting on the brown leather couch with wide space and angles, Julian disclosed his worry that I might hurt myself during my panic attacks. Trying to put his mind at ease, I stated I had no intentions of hurting myself.

"How am I supposed to know, Momma Llama?"

Great question. He should never have to guess, should he?

"Right now, I'm in a good place, Jug Bug. I am healing. Those thoughts are not in my mind these days," I said, smiling. "We're gonna be OK."

"I love you, Momma."

"I know, buddy, and I receive it! I love you too." We hugged.

Julian was not 100 percent convinced of my safety. Unfortunately, he knew about the haunting demonic darkness that's threatened to take my life for decades. I'll be straight here: I never expected to live this long.

Troubleshooting later that afternoon with Michele, we went over the mess, especially my talk with Julian, when she exclaimed something profoundly life-altering in a matter-of-fact, loving tone: "Tell him that suicide is off the table, Leigh! It's not an option for you any longer."

"How do you know?" I was completely confused.

"Suicide is a primitive strategy." Michele went on to remind me I had developed better tools.

"Yes," then, voiced desperately, I asked "How do you know I won't resort to it?" I badly needed reassurance that she really did know.

"Because, Leigh, you're no longer hopeless and desperate. You understand your past, your abuse, the reasons behind the pain, and you've worked through them with your therapist. You are working to replace negative emotions and the abuse they are tied to with positive ones. You know the abuse and neglect are not your fault. You no longer have any reason to kill yourself. Take suicide off the table for yourself and Julian." Sternly convicting in a way I welcomed, my godly mentor sounded how I imagine an old ox would sound wisely directing a younger one furrowing fields under the same yoke.

She plowed on, "Tell him he checks in with you ONCE to make sure that being left alone is really what you want. You get one chance to change your mind now. But it's only once, and you both understand this. Then he's off the hook."

Yes, ma'am!

You have no idea what relief hearing this was, worth every torture chamber experience this journey had unearthed. With shackles falling from my wrists crashing onto concrete floors, I purposefully marched out of that prison holding keys for unlocking Julian's adjoining jail cell too.

Beelining for Julian's room to celebrate the great news that suicide was off the table, I beheld how one promise released the weight of enormous responsibility I'd unwittingly placed upon my son, like Atlas dropping the earth off his shoulders. With his worry-guilt handcuff unlocked, Julian's countenance changed, and I saw freedom rising for the next generation.

The following Monday, my therapist shared an interesting agreement she makes with self-harm patients the first six months of EMDR sessions to remove the suicide option for half a year because of suicide's incompatibility with therapy's goals of healing. After patients have undergone EMDR therapy that long, she noted that suicidal tendencies often disappear.

I was inclined to agree.

Suicide, you can go straight back from whence you came—to hell. I'm drop-kicking you out the window. NO Christmas card for YOU. You're officially OFF THE LIST!

Verses to Consider

Psalm 51:1–19
Psalm 139
Isaiah 61:1

She Seems So Normal podcast

Chapter 19

LESSON FIVE: DEVELOP VULNERABILITY, CULTIVATE COURAGE

"Hoping your story will give me courage to finish my own."

An author/speaker friend wrote this to me after I told her about this book's premise. Originally, I meant to share it as a warning of the hard stories and ideas she'd encounter and since "she seemed so normal," her response surprised me. Who knew this beautiful, pulled-together lady had dark topics like depression and surviving bad parenting waiting in the wings like me? You would never know it looking at her.

I told her, "Brené Brown says courage is contagious, so you can borrow some of mine if I can borrow yours when I need it![1] –xoxo."

Feeling the Lord pressing my heart to share was the main reason for publishing my story. However, an equally compelling component was watching Simone Biles and the Olympic gymnasts offer their abuse testimony before Congress. Crying on my couch holding rescue dogs Scout and Louie, I held my breath as each athlete took her turn answering intimate, uncomfortable questions at the hearing. At times, I whispered, "Yes, sister, be brave and courageous. It has to stop." Witnessing others bravely standing up to speak inspired me. Watching the Weinstein, Epstein, Lauer, Cosby, and Hefner stories and the rest of their grotesque predator group emerging as front-page news, I marveled yet again at the ones who stopped the collective collateral damage and stood up to these modern-day Midianites.

 ## God Loves the Underdog

47

Oh, how God loves underdogs! God constantly chooses and uses "least of these" kinda people, like Rahab the Jericho prostitute to help Joshua's spies, unschooled fishermen, money-grubbing tax collectors, political zealots, "crazy" dudes eating locusts and wearing camel-hair cloaks preaching in rivers, and doubting disciples to spread the gospel to the furthest reaches of the known world. Only when these unlikelies owned and aligned with God's narrative did they overcome and shatter their fears. Vulnerability is powerful.

As we wholly align with God's purposeful calling, yielding and listening for His voice to be the one we hear, defeat is not an option, no matter how much of an underdog we are. I love how God helps develop our courage with every persevering step through the valley. As we intimately reveal the true state of our souls to Him by exposing our deepest fears, He proves Himself reliable and trustworthy, an incomparable ally.

Gideon's victory over the Midianites in Judges 6–8 is an Old Testament example. God first called this "mighty warrior" while he was threshing wheat in a winepress and grumbling about history and prophecies (Judges 6:13).

Claiming he was from the weakest Israelite clan and the least of his family (Judge 6:15), Gideon obediently provided a traditional guest meal offering to the angel of the Lord and was shocked when fire from heaven consumed dinner right in front of him.

When the Lord instructed Gideon to tear down two major altars of false worship in his hometown, repurpose the wood for a proper altar, and burn a sacrifice to Yahweh on it, Gideon was afraid of what his family and the townspeople might do in response. With crickets chirping and chickens rustling on roosts, the mighty warrior completed God's instructions by the light of the moon, repurposing the despised Asherah pole, demolishing the detestable altar of Ba'al, and sacrificing a bull as a burnt offering. He declared the newly built altar *Jehovah Shalom* ("the Lord is peace"). Awakening the following morning to smells of fresh-cut wood and roast beef wafting through the streets, the townspeople discovered Gideon's deed. They demanded he die until Gideon's father spoke wisdom, turning them away from their murderous task.

While Israel's deadliest enemies camped and gathered forces at Jezreel by the Jordan River, the Spirit of God prompted Gideon to do something brave. Sounding the trumpet, Gideon heralded a call to arms, and thirty-two thousand men assembled. Gideon, still seemingly half-hearted about initiating battle and concerned about following God's plan, took two nights to request those famous sheepskin fleece confirmations.

Does it seem like courage came in increments the more Gideon obeyed? Yeah.

After God winnowed his forces from tens of thousands to three hundred fearless, dog-lapping soldiers with borrowed provisions and trumpets, Gideon must have been filled with doubt again. So God told him to go into enemy territory to eavesdrop on the retelling of a soldier's barley bread nightmare.

With this final confirmation firmly fixed in his frontal cortex, Gideon gained courage and vision. With just three hundred men, God (through Gideon) destroyed 120,000 Midianites to win the day.

Allowing ourselves permission to be vulnerable, unprotected, and exposed when the Holy Spirit calls is scary, but this is seemingly when God performs His finest work through us. We're not called to do anything in our own power; when we trust in the indwelling resources we have in Christ, His grace is sufficient and His power is made perfect in our weakness. When we are weak, we are strong (2 Corinthians 12:9–10). When we stop succumbing to pride and depending on our personal power to serve the kingdom, we are blessed to inherit the earth (Matthew 5:5). Just ask the ladies of the Gospels.

Nothing Shows Our True Colors Better Than Witnessing
48

Nowhere are our true colors more evident than in our response to poverty, authentic worship, and suffering. How we react to these reveals who we really are.

Poverty. For many women in traditional Eastern cultures around the world, becoming a widow is a terrifying prospect. After women marry, their husbands, rather than their families of origin, provide financial security and physical protection. No husband and no sons often mean no safety. While teaching in eastern India with CARE India, I met beautiful Venkatamma. With few teeth, many wrinkles, and leprosy-ravaged stumps for hands and feet, she invited me into her sparse, humble tenement that was swept clean with pride. Earlier during Communion, I witnessed her carefully balance bread and a precious cup of juice atop her flesh-eaten hands, reverently receiving the body and blood of Christ with praise and gratitude. As my words were translated from English to Telugu, I marveled about her lovely home, thanking her for blessing me in church. I noticed she was bony beneath her sari as we gently hugged. I silently wondered how long it'd been since another human held her close, touched her skin, or looked into her eyes.

In Mark 12, while the rich made grand gestures of gifting shekels upon shekels of gold and silver to the temple treasury, Jesus noticed the widow with copper coins. (I think of Venkatamma.) With His disciples close, He recognized her true, unconstrained offering of faith from the depths of her heart. In contrast, He confronted the rich young ruler in Luke 18 to forsake his heart-state idolatry of holding on to his wealth, which kept him from a greater eternal treasure in heaven.

Jesus noticed the impoverished and the untouchable castoffs. He saw me—spiritually impoverished and emotionally outcast—and brought me close to change my heart.

Worship. People show their true colors in the presence of someone's most unguarded, intimate worship moments. Much to the red-hot irritation and dismay of her sister, Mary not only sat meekly at Jesus's feet to absorb His teaching, one night she washed them too. While she was willing to humbly scrub dirt from His soles just days before His death, others gave her grief for wasting the expensive nard oil she used to anoint him. The transparent light of this unfiltered, loving act of worship prompted a greedy, green-faced thief, Judas, to betray

Jesus to the religious leaders, who blacklisted their competition for destruction.

What keeps us from unrestrained worship? Wanting to fit in with the crowd or feeling self-conscious, intimidated, or embarrassed, afraid of judgment or being "too much" or "too weird." What shades identify our true colors in God's eyes?

Suffering. Jesus crucified at Golgotha, in misery, moaning and crying and dying, insults and sin hurled, with thorns, spears, and nails stuck in His flesh—who stayed near to witness the end and beyond, who wept and longed for His life till His last breath? Those familiar with pain and marginalization: the women. Shrouded in sadness, they performed the dirtiest, most thankless ministry work sitting with and watching the suffering of the Savior. The testimonies of these women would never have been accepted in a court of law. They traipsed quietly across cobblestone on the dawn of that third day to serve the Lord's earthly ministry one last time. Imagine the surprise and joy of being the first to receive the most precious reward of all time—one that kings and prophets wrote about and longed to see—the risen Christ! The first to proclaim witness, they provided us the pioneer testimony to the resurrection of the King.

How do we embrace others who are emotionally, physically, or spiritually exposed? How do we care for the vulnerable? As we walk alongside one another as believers, the level of suffering or shame we will shoulder measures our courage to embody God's compassionate character when it comes to "messy." Many times, there's nothing to say, but simply being present, available, and willing to embrace the lonely and lovingly serve God and one another through the challenges makes all the difference. Who knows what reward awaits us in the end?

> *Vulnerability is our most accurate measure of courage.*
> *. . . Vulnerability is being all in.*

—Brené Brown, *Power of Vulnerability*

Do a New Thing

49   Here's the ultimate narrative exposure. We've all done bad things. Everyone has fallen short of perfection and needs saving. God knew it would happen even as far back as the first forbidden, crunch-swallowed fruit. When He slaughtered the animals, spilling their blood over the grass and stones, God covered Adam and Eve's "oops, we didn't listen" sin. Later, after bringing Abraham, Isaac, and Jacob's descendants out of Egyptian slavery through Moses, the Lord established the covenant with His people (Exodus 19) and gave behavior basics in the Ten Commandments (Exodus 20) at Mount Sinai.

Throughout the history of Israel, when the people pleaded and needed to be saved from the torment of bully nations and ruthless tribes, God sent judges, prophets, or kings. The people cheered and praised God, then quickly forgot Him again. The cycle repeated through centuries. Empires rose and fell. Israel was taken into captivity by the Assyrians and Judah by the Babylonians. Those kingdoms fell. Then came the Persians. And theirs fell. And then, in the fullness of time, as Rome rose to world-power status, "The Word became flesh and made his dwelling among us. We have seen his glory, the glory of the one and only Son, who came from the Father, full of grace and truth" (John 1:14).

Jesus. He came to save humanity.

I think one of the bravest, most inspiring things in the world is doing a 180, pivoting in the opposite direction. When we recognize something isn't working and are willing to turn around to start from scratch, building the beautiful with the basic and bare-boned elements we have within our grasp can be a mighty work of God.

In the Old Testament, the Bible talks about new mercies (Lamentations 3), new songs (Psalm 40:3), a new covenant (Jeremiah 30), and a new heart (Ezekiel 36:26). Do these still hold true in the New Testament? Of course!

In John 3, stars glimmered as Nicodemus, a prominent Pharisee on the Jewish ruling council, came for a midnight message about the kingdom of God. When Jesus explained about being born again, the wise old man was distressed, prompting the question, "How can someone be born when they are old? . . . Surely, they cannot enter a second time into their mother's womb to be born!" (v. 4).

Jesus explained that true spiritual renewal comes only through a new birth and the baptism and indwelling of the Spirit of God. Nicodemus needed something new; he was desperate to know what. He just needed Jesus.

As the Savior ministered openly step-by-step toward his final journey to Jerusalem in what would become His ultimate sacrifice at the cross, Nicodemus developed conviction, commitment, and courageousness to challenge the chief priests and Pharisees in John 7:51: "Does our law condemn a man without first hearing him to find out what he has been doing?" He was slapped down and silenced by the snappy spiritual cynicism of his superiors.

Twelve chapters later, though, at the end of Good Friday, Nicodemus was with Joseph of Arimathea, who requested Christ's broken body from Pilate, using his personal resources to honor the Lord at his own unused tomb (John 19:39). If that courage, birthed from a fifteen-minute honest, intimate conversation with the Savior, could change Nicodemus, what could it do for us?

When Jesus shed his sinless blood for sinful humanity, His arms opened wide on the cross, compelling all to come to and through Him. From the criminally convicted to the religiously respected, all come to God the same way: by faith in Jesus. And all can have new life, a new birth, forgiveness, and a new heavenly home.

I experienced this. It changed my life.

If you have never met the Master or felt the forgiveness that He alone can give, you can do it today. Through the cross, Jesus completed the work of soul salvation to provide you a heavenly eternity. The only thing left to do is to surrender your life by faith and begin following Him right now.[2]

> If you declare with your mouth, "Jesus is Lord," and believe in your heart that God raised him from the dead, you will be saved. . . . for, "Everyone who calls on the name of the Lord will be saved." (Romans 10:9, 13)

Own It

I love me some Brené Brown, who says you will either own your story or hustle for worthiness, and owning our stories helps us avoid getting trapped as characters in stories someone else is telling.[3] She also teaches that shame grows in secrecy, silence, and judgment, but compassion is a shame killer.

My entire life was spent hustling for worthiness. I was desperate for signs and accolades to show I wasn't a waste of oxygen. No matter the accomplishment, how well I did, what I had, or who I influenced, it was never enough to fill the bottomless abyss. I was the character in someone else's story. Until now.

Now, my story is owned outright. You're presently reading the new ending of the narrative. I will unapologetically work against my shame and the shame of others, staunchly refuse to people-please or disappear, and actively fight to maintain authenticity and vulnerability.

Do you know someone with shame? Brené's research says empathy is the cure.

Maybe reading this book is the key to overcoming your shame. Maybe it's the key to unlocking empathy for someone else. Can we make this world a better place for those with trauma? I think we can. What happens when we develop vulnerability and embrace courage? We get to choose the endings to our stories.

Verses to Consider

Judges 6–8
Psalm 40:3
Jeremiah 30
Lamentations 3
Ezekiel 36:26
John 3:7, 19

She Seems So Normal podcast

LESSON SIX: YOU HAVE
THE POWER TO CHOOSE

Men and women who live Wholeheartedly
DIG Deep. . . .DELIBERATE in their thoughts
and behaviors through prayer, meditation, or simply
setting their intentions; INSPIRED to make new and
different choices; GOING. They take action.

—Brené Brown, *The Gifts of Imperfection*

Ever heard, "She can't help it; it's just the way she was raised?" or "The whole family's a mess; they're just born that way"?

For those in the back of the room, let me say it again: origin stories are important for understanding why and how we are the way we are. It helps us understand and identify programming and the beliefs that drive our actions and behaviors when we know the auspices under which we've been raised, our genetic predispositions, or generational family narratives.

Wanna know what's more important than an origin story? Choice.

Made in the image of God and given free will from the beginning, as individuals and nations, we can choose between life and death, blessings and curses (Deuteronomy 30:19). We're given choices between obedience and disobedience, following Christ or our own selfish worldly desires, believing God or the d'Evil.

For years, voices from the past may have shouted every negative comment and echoed in my mind, but I allowed them to reinfect the way I thought again and again until I realized something: I have the power to choose.

How many voices compete for the microphone in your headspace? Who's the loudest? We can decide to think differently.

Let's pray for the Holy Spirit to have the only microphone and speak the only discernible message between our ears, whether it's in a thunderclap or a still, small whisper.

When God breathed His Spirit and breath into the dirt-man Adam, he began to live. After Adam and his wife chose to believe the serpent and ate the fruit, God covered that original sin and nakedness, too, with the flesh of the animals He created. He'd later cover the origin story of sin with the body and blood of His Son.

Origin stories are important, but we still get to make choices. I chose to break my plastic-princess mold and be different from how I was raised or groomed. You can too.

Words Matter (Flowers and Weeds)

I am learning to love
the sound of my feet
walking away from things
not meant for me

—Unknown

Words are seeds, growing flowers and weeds.

Has someone ever made a comment you took to heart and allowed to shape you? All of us have at one time or another been inspired or destroyed by the power of words. Sticks and stones can break bones, but *wowee!* watch out for the names that destroy you.

When I was young, so many thoughts were implanted into Little Me. That happened to all of us. The difference is the types of seeds that were planted and how we grew them.

Some seeds thrown at us fall off and can't get under our skin. It's the ones that land and we nurse over time that matter. We fertilize and grow these by repeating them to ourselves over and over again.

It's like being stung by a wasp. The initial time really, really hurts, but if you're stung again and again, you go numb from the pain. Or you die of the poison.

That is the power of words.

James, the half brother of Jesus, said it best when he wrote about taming the tongue. It is a restless evil, full of poison that is deadly, and it sets forests on fire with just a small spark: "The tongue also is a fire, a world of evil among the parts of the body. It corrupts the whole body, sets the whole course of one's life on fire, and is itself set on fire by hell" (James 3:6).

We can change a lot in our lives when we begin to watch the words we speak and what we say to ourselves. We can choose to take every thought captive and make it obedient to Christ (2 Corinthians 10:5). We measure our thoughts against the truth of Scripture and the character of God.

This is the greater power of His Word.

Hey! Change How You Pray

38   Sometimes you just gotta speak things into existence and change the words you use about yourself and others. This seems like something God will keep teaching me again and again until I'll get it. In the fall of 2019, He taught me to change how I pray.

See, I used to pray things like, "Thank you, God, for loving me even though I am a wretched, horrible woman. I don't understand your mercy and grace for such a sinner like me! Why do you even bother with me, Lord? Thank you for loving me."

While this is a true statement and, in a sense, I believe it, do you see what I now see? It's a self-centered and self-defeating way to pray if it is my norm. Stabbing myself in the heart each time I pray also puts the emphasis on me instead of on praising God.

What I've noticed is that this prayer utters a half-truth. I'm covered in the blood of His Son; God doesn't hate and love me at the same time. While He despises and hates the sin, He loves the sinner.

This was the preprogrammed banter that started my every prayer throughout the entire day. It's hate filled for one who is beloved of the King, and I would never, ever speak this way before the Lord about anyone else. It's a flat-out self-destructive mindset.

Have you ever needed to reprogram your words and use different phrases and descriptors? Yeah, me too. It's usually when we are alerted and become more sensitive to how others' feelings need to be affirmed instead of dismissed. When we know better, we do better.

I realized the words of this first prayer not only beat

me up emotionally and spiritually, but they also dishonored the work the Father had done in me to this point. While I'm still a sinner until I go home to heaven, I've also got to recognize and honor what God loves, which is His image and His redemption in me.

I think of the verses where we are told to encourage one another in Scripture:

1. "Therefore encourage one another and build each other up" (1 Thessalonians 5:11).
2. "But encourage one another daily, as long as it is called 'Today,' so that none of you may be hardened by sin's deceitfulness" (Hebrews 3:13).
3. "Finally, brothers and sisters, rejoice! Strive for full restoration, encourage one another, be of one mind, live in peace" (2 Corinthians 13:11).

While I was perhaps good encouragement to those around me, I had rarely encouraged myself in a truly godly way. Instead, what I did was spiritually poke myself with a stick. I mean, Jesus saw the thief being crucified on the cross next to him, loved him and didn't despise him, and promised that man eternity. Doesn't He love me like that too?

Loved and Despised

While we're at it, let's think about this: I'm my own sister in Christ. Would I ever pray like this for someone else? Never. You wouldn't, either.

Here's what Isaiah 43, verses 1 and 4 say: "Do not fear, for I have redeemed you; I have summoned you by name; you are mine. . . . Since you are precious and honored in my sight, and because I love you, I will give people in exchange for you, nations in exchange for your life."

I know He was talking about Israel, but I believe He's speaking to me too. The Lord is with me as He draws me into these deep waters and through the rivers I am crossing, especially when I think I'm going to drown in them. I'm crying as I write this, feeling His overwhelming love for me.

My God has never left or abandoned me. He loves me so much, and even more than that, He created me to be not just likable but lovable to others!

Does this seem obvious? It was a revelation to me. I had no idea until one Sunday God whispered His message of my lovability in my ear. Like a giant serpent winding around its prey, an enormous lie had gripped me from the beginning of my walk with Jesus and kept its stranglehold on me.

What Was the Lie?

In the Father's eyes, I believed I was simultaneously loved *and* despised. What I realize now was part of the predatory sexual/emotional abuse cycle, for the abused to be both the object of love and derision is not actually love at all—it's wrong and sinful and psychotic. And it does not reflect God's perfect love.

Gosh, how sick is that? I'm not sure if anyone ever made this connection for me out loud before right now as I type. Self-hatred is real; how many of us come before the Father with this crazy view of ourselves? We receive the love and affection of God while also condemning ourselves as unworthy, maybe feeling like impostors, as the serpent urges us on to believe we are despised objects of wrath. We, as the beloved children of Yahweh, stay in those cages afraid and arrested in our spiritual lives and growth.

Once God begins unraveling a lie, though, I find myself catching a breath of the truth, and that truth is setting me free.

Ahhhhh! When and how does this cycle end?

It ends with the truth of Scripture.

In the words of Forrest Gump, I know what love is. My husband and other true friends role-model agape (godly love). I recognize it because I see sacrificial Christ-likeness in their interactions with me. It's that 1 Corinthians 13 kind of love that is patient and kind, humble and honoring. It's not selfish, dishonest, or easily angered, and it sure doesn't keep a record of wrongs or delight in evil but rejoices in the truth. Real agape love protects, trusts, hopes, and perseveres in Jesus Christ even when I don't deserve it or recognize it. And agape love isn't for show or earthly reward; it is given simply because this is how God calls us to love one another.

👑 The Prayer of Someone Who Is Loved and
39 Lovable

> *Thank you, Father, for loving me and creating me to be lovable. Help me to overcome these lies. Your almighty power and glory are overwhelming, and I bow down at the throne before you. Jesus, thank you that you protect me from wrath by your blood. Lord, light me on fire like your burning ones! Light my soul on fire with your love!*

You have no idea how hard this chapter was for me to write, to receive so many huge revelations in such a small space of time. It wore me out so much I had to step away for a bit, taking some time to reflect on how much more in love with Jesus I've become. I also needed some space to breathe and call in prayer warriors.

I'm so grateful for my small but mighty tribe spread all over the world. I can call on them anytime for support. Here was the first sweet prayer text I received: "Leigh, in the name of the Mighty One, may the God who is with us always be so near that you feel His hand on your shoulder. Peace, my sister."

The second text was Allison praying Isaiah 12.

In that day you will say:

> "I will praise you, LORD.
> 	Although you were angry with me,
> your anger has turned away
> 	and you have comforted me.
> Surely God is my salvation;
> 	I will trust and not be afraid.
> The LORD, the LORD himself, is my strength and
> 		my defense;
> 	he has become my salvation."
> With joy you will draw water
> 	from the wells of salvation.

In that day you will say:

> "Give praise to the LORD, proclaim his name;
> 	make known among the nations what he has done,
> 	and proclaim that his name is exalted.
> Sing to the LORD, for he has done glorious things;

let this be known to all the world.
Shout aloud and sing for joy, people of Zion,
    for great is the Holy One of Israel
        among you."

The Lord himself is my strength and my defense; he has become my salvation. I will give praise and song, exalting and proclaiming your name, my God! I will make known among the nations the glorious things that you've done. O Holy One, you are good, and you are great. *Selah.*

Shake It Off—I Don't Have to Do This Anymore

Spring sunlight blinked and sparkled as green grass vibrantly pulsated in the breeze. The blossoming star magnolia waved outside the window as I stood at the kitchen counter stirring half-and-half into my coffee, contentedly watching Christopher work.

From nowhere, an intrusive event image fluttered into my mind, barging through the floor-to-ceiling plate-glass windows of my home. The face, the "Red Room" panic.

"No!" I said, muttering. "You can't push me around anymore! This is a beautiful day, and you're not ruining it." I literally put my hands up to bat the memory away from my brain and body.

And you know what? It went away.

I have the power to make it leave; I can choose to refuse to let it haunt me anymore. We must take captive every thought and make it obedient to Christ. Holy Spirit power lives and resides inside of me. I think I finally understand that I can rebuke the enemy, resist him, and he will flee. Roaring lions cannot devour me in this area anymore. I. Am. Free.

I am so pleased with how far I've come. We conquered the Red Room, for Pete's sake! It doesn't scare me anymore.

Oh, the comfort and peace of monumental breakthroughs:

- I am not worthless; my life is of great value. #BloodOfChrist
- I am worthy of respect, kindness, and good things. #ImageOfGod
- I am not to blame for the abuse that happened to me as a child. #TruthOfChrist
- I am deserving of love. #ChildOfGod

I. Am. Still. Standing.
The fear of this memory—gone.
The knives I used to stab myself—gone.
The emotional slicing and dicing—gone.
The physical manifestations—gone.

The body does keep the score, but mine no longer has to remember it.

Verses to Consider

Isaiah 12
Isaiah 43:1, 4
1 Corinthians 13
2 Corinthians 10:5
James 3:6

She Seems So Normal podcast

Chapter 21

LESSON SEVEN: SACRED SPHERES OF SUPPORT

I believe that vulnerability—the willingness to show up and be seen with no guarantee of outcome—is the only path to more love, belonging, and joy.

—Brené Brown, *Rising Strong*

The Courage to Heal in Community

In her book *Daring Greatly*, Brené Brown says, "Shame derives its power from being unspeakable."[1] Isn't that the truth? The enemy is like a roving lion, isolating his prey to kill in silence.

The higher our influence (think: church, work, community, politics, or online), the harder it becomes to show chinks in our armor. Fear of being stabbed by competitive ladder climbers is real, especially for thought pioneers and visionary leaders. Additionally, when framed within a picture book of past abuse scenarios, even a smidgen of betrayal embellishes shame-pain in particularly exquisite and, at times, practically intolerable ways to reinforce old cycles and unhelpful thought patterns.

My farm-girl brain remembers barnyard references in Scripture. Matthew 7 is the one about not giving dogs what's sacred or throwing pearls to pigs lest they trample the most precious of all jewelry under their stinky split-hooves or turn and shred you with rabid teeth.

We need BOUNDARIES.[2] We shouldn't expose our struggles to or share our fears with everyone, or ask them to shoulder our pain and heartbreak. However, without accountability and fellowship, if we don't seek godly help, nothing changes. Lacking spiritual oxygen, without movement, our faith stagnates like pond water in a hot, dry summer.

How do we develop safe spheres of support to find trustworthy people who have earned the right to hear our deepest and darkest secrets and kill self-inflicting shame?

Healing in community is hard and holy work requiring that the people around us be set apart by the Holy Spirit. As you've seen throughout this narrative, prayerfully recognizing the who, the how, the where, and the when of openness was the key for developing my spheres of trust and accountability.

Let's be courageous to speak what's unspeakable, shall we?

♛ Overcome Shame
40

Sitting in Bible study fifteen years ago, I was amazed my church hadn't been struck by lightning the moment I walked in. *If only these nice church women knew what I'd done in the past, they wouldn't be so welcoming. They would toss me out the first chance they got.*

Hiding like a plastic-princess zebra in her dazzle,[3] I camouflaged all my issues to blend into the landscape. But the longer I spent in Scripture, the more I felt like an impostor in church, realizing the paint I'd colored my stripes with turned wonky chameleon colors under the glow of the Son. In the meantime, the enemy loved reminding me what I used to be like, and so I was often pulled in two directions—knowing Christ's grace, forgiveness, and mercy yet listening to lies, condemnation, and accusations. If we are trying to cover disobedience or hide pre-Jesus deeds, our peace will rarely last long as we wonder at what moment our sin will find us out (Numbers 32:23) and we'll be exposed as the frauds we are.

Recently, I heard my pastor, Jeanne Stevens,[4] offer a clever acronym for the word **SHAME**: **S**elf-**H**atred **A**t **M**y **E**xpense.

Boy, did she nail it!

Shame *is* self-inflicted, self-infecting, self-absorbing, and self-hating. It submits way too MUCH power to "self" while trusting way too little in JESUS. Overcoming "me" meant confronting past issues face-to-face, no matter how uncomfortable it made me or my trusted circle feel.

As you read throughout parts 1 and 2, my intentional awareness of processing and confessing the guilt of disobedience, rebellion, and unfaithfulness to God prompted me to continuously ask hard questions and wait on biblically sound answers through daily Scripture reading, prayer, and accountability with close friends and mentors. Other courageous measures I took included marching into professional therapy;

seeking wisdom from my spiritual teachers and leaders; carefully curating safe spaces filled with trusted, wise counsel; and refusing to shrink back at the taunts of a cowardly lion.

Under Holy Spirit inspiration, the beloved disciple John penned the final book of the Bible while imprisoned on a desert island after extended solo worship time in a cave. Through him, the Bible is clear how we triumph and how a hurled-down d'Evil retreats through this revolutionary revelation:

> For the accuser of our brothers and sisters,
>> who accuses them before our God day and night,
>> has been hurled down.
> They triumphed over him
>> by the blood of the Lamb
>> and by the word of their testimony;
> they did not love their lives so much
>> as to shrink from death.
>
> (Revelation 12:10–11)

Did you see it? As Christ followers, we triumph by the blood of Jesus *and* our testimony, no matter how death-filled or intimidating our circumstances seem.

Unlearn Unhealthy Thought Cycles

Predatory grooming is difficult to overcome. For trauma and abuse survivors, the temptation to isolate is instinctive. We're programmed by abusers to keep secrets, instilled with a belief that seeking help won't change anything, so our darkness grows. The roaring lion continues devouring when we resist humility by stubbornly gripping anxieties close instead of casting them away, not trusting that God will lift us up in due time.

It's prideful to think that the omnipotent, omnipresent, and omniscient God who created all things can't save us.

That's a weird thought. Can those who've been abused be prideful?

Even if abuse isn't your background, you've probably kept secrets. Ever compared your troubles and struggles with others thinking your suffering wasn't as bad? So you kept quiet and didn't seek help. Maybe you just kept taking whatever "it" is, thinking longsuffering is godly.

At what point does absorbing or unleashing painful words or deeds become abusive? Enabling? Are we fixing a loved one's problems ourselves or keeping them from suffering the natural consequences of bad behavior?

My prayer tribe is vigilant; I do my best to keep them informed, giving permission for my close friends, my battle buddies, to call me out if they see me in shame, unhealthy thought cycles, or isolation. It's so easy to slip back into old habits without accountability.

Community is a godly provision that we have the power to enact. My husband, kids, girlfriends, and the people in my neighborhoods of influence have been sources of enormous support as I've become bolder about sharing my journey. My church is a multitude of blessings from leadership to biblical teaching and serving opportunities.

We were never meant to do this walk alone, friend. Right now, take back the blood-bought power of the Holy Spirit. Stand on the battlefield as we fight for the kingdom together.

Four things:

1. Look around: Who speaks truth and godly encouragement for you right now?

2. Gather trustworthy support.

3. What message, experience, or other special way can you support someone in need?

4. Is there a "messy" person in your life God assigned for you to help? Don't give up on them—I am practically begging you!—please do not give up on the person God sent you to help.

With pom-poms to spare, I'm here cheering YOU on from the other side of this shadow-death valley. Can you see the lady jumping, smiling, and waving? That's me.

All I ask: once you cross, turn around and help cheer on the next one in the valley cuz soon there could be an army of us shouting, "Keep going! You can do it!"

His Hand Covers Mine—I Am "Precious" (4.25.2020)

Approaching my appointment, I wasn't sure where to start. There wasn't really anything further I needed or wanted to know about the past. When I texted Michele, she reminded me I need not relive every single encounter or trauma event to know what I need to know. It was reassuring to finally know enough to grasp the issues I'd been facing. As I continued to heal, more of my memories came back, but I was now equipped with resources and help. As the adult, I could decide what to do, and if I needed help, people could give me a hand.

My plan was to say farewell to my therapist; however, that wasn't God's plan. We ended up covering the most important human relationship I have: my husband.

With gobs of transparency and mascara running down my cheeks, I confessed to the times I wanted to run away, leave Christopher to start fresh, and vanish from the earth, reasoning if I left, our kids could have a better, less-damaged mom and my husband could have a worthy wife.

Taking note of words I used, *worthless, unworthy of him, he deserved better than me*, my therapist repeated them back, asking me more about them. By the end of our time, she asked how I would rather feel, so I told her I would much rather feel beloved and that my life has purpose, that I wanted to feel precious. Yes. Precious.

Did you know the word *precious* is used forty-eight times in Scripture?[5] Along with describing stones and pearls, it also describes faith, God's promises, Christ's blood, Jesus as the cornerstone, and the children of Zion. What does it mean, though?

The Enhanced Brown-Driver-Briggs Hebrew and English Lexicon says the word is rendered *yāqar* in the ancient text, and like every Hebrew word, its meaning is multilayered.[6] To be "precious" is to be prized or appraised as heavy or with weight, honored, costly, or splendid. The crux of the issue, the word for me, what my soul longs to believe!

Later that evening, Christopher and I pillow-talked to process the day.

"You really love me, don't you?" I asked.

As I looked into his eyes tearfully, he smiled back. "You know I do."

Reflecting on my morning therapy session, I blurted out, "I just want to feel precious, but I don't know how!" Honestly, I had no idea what that meant. My "precious" was stolen in a Red Room. Or when my father left. Or even before that at birth.

My hand gripped in a fist of frustration. Tears came in earnest, and my face contorted into that ugly "smile reassuringly while feeling like your heart is twisting in your ribs" look.

Christopher placed his warm hand over my fist, triggering a remote memory of being tiny, vulnerable, and sad. I closed my eyes to see a Holy Spirit–inspired vision, a Salvador Dalí-esque painting of two hands floating in space. Mine, a chubby, pale baby hand, was wrapped inside one giant and strong—the hand of God. A rainbow-hued warmth emanated between this digit connection, pulsated, and eclipsed my chunky hand to become a bright sphere sitting atop an enormous open palm. *Precious*, the word echoes. *You ARE precious*, Father repeats.

"I am precious," I echoed absently and opened my eyes. Christopher was still cradling my fist. I understood it. Finally.

The reckless narrative I had written over this relationship for more than thirty years, the one wrongly proclaiming *I am worthless*, kept defeating and unraveling the fabric of our marriage time and time again. Believing the enemy's lie of my unworthiness, feeling Christopher deserved better, caused me to throw a thousand Molotov cocktails in sabotage attempts to force an opt-out divorce, yet my husband stayed, fighting each fire. I could not understand, until suddenly I did.

Love conquers all. Remember 1 Corinthians 13? That says it all.

It also fits Christopher to a tee. With this singular heartfelt action, he has communicated that I am precious, costly, and worthy of honor and splendor because God sees his wife with utter and complete love.

God held out this sacred, saving gift to me and placed it in the palm of Christopher's hand. I will never forget such a beautiful lesson. Never.

> *For he will deliver the needy who cry out, the afflicted*
> *who have no one to help. He will take pity on the weak*
> *and the needy and save the needy from death.*
> *He will rescue them from oppression and violence,*
> *for precious is their blood in his sight.*
> —Psalm 72:12–14

Verses to Consider
Psalm 72:12–14
2 Corinthians 13:4–8
Revelation 12:10–11

She Seems So Normal podcast

For more funny animal names

Chapter 22

LESSON EIGHT: FORGIVENESS IS THE KEY TO THE KINGDOM

Restoration and Reconciliation

58

It was early December 2020. Since that summer, my son had been at college in Chicago. We had suffered multiple deaths of (be)loved ones and had a few huge shifts in ministry. Waiting for an opportune time, I could not catch a good opening to speak to extended family about what transpired in therapy.

It's not like I hadn't tried; it's just every time, it was shut down or glossed over, and we quickly moved on to other topics. Discussing trauma therapy is like COVID-19: cover your face, put on your mask, don't touch anything or anyone, and repeatedly sanitize and wash your hands ASAP so you don't bring it into your home. It's dangerous and we don't know who it's gonna kill or who's getting through unscathed. The problem? No one gets through it unscathed—everyone is traumatized.

In November, with as much courage as I could muster, Christopher and I along with Michele and my therapist strategized the process to share the burden of knowledge with and offer loving confrontation, forgiveness, and

215

reconciliation to my family. Literally empowered by a graphic of all possible responses and why they didn't matter, I even had the words written I would say if it came to that. Prepared for a hurricane backlash and all the worst-case scenarios, we bathed ourselves in prayer and God's Word.

A preformatted, proofed email received approval on all sides from professionals and pastoral support while giving appropriate honor, love, and hope without mincing words about the source of my childhood sexual abuse. I offered my family of origin the opportunity to schedule time to Zoom or call with questions, initially thinking we would videoconference everyone with Christopher as my rescue agent. In case anything went sideways, he would end the call, protecting and extracting me.

My main goals were explaining what had happened and forgiving any known or unknown roles in the abuse, whether from ignorance, complicit enabling, or actively allowing it. My main message was first and foremost to emphasize Christ's love and forgiveness because they are what matter, not mine.

My mother kept her cards close on what she knew or didn't know. She simply wished me well in my struggles and hoped the best for me. What I realize now is that she probably didn't have the bandwidth or the tools to fully enter the conversation. This makes me wonder about my mom's own trauma stories. Knowing she, too, was groomed by the perpetrators around us, I've asked various times if she was ever abused, but she has denied it. I wonder if, like me, God blessed her with amnesia.

My dad was shocked. Since he wasn't around, he had no idea, and he apologized profusely. How could he know their divorce would lead to such abuse or leave such long-lasting, unforeseeable scars?

For my abusers—the groomers, child molesters, and rapists masquerading as live-in boyfriends, babysitters' husbands, baseball coaches, banished businessmen, or brazen brothers-in-arms—is there a place for predators in heaven or absolution for abusers? C. S. Lewis said,

> I do not think that all who choose wrong roads perish; but their rescue consists in being put back on the right road. A wrong sum can be put right: but only by going back till you find the error and working it afresh from that point, never by simply *going on*. Evil can be undone, but it cannot "develop" into good. Time does not heal it. The spell must be unwound, bit by bit, "with backward mutters of dissevering power"—or else not.[1]

I didn't come to my conclusions about abusers because of C. S. Lewis. I found it in my walk with Jesus, but this quote is a good explanation for others' understanding.

The space I hold in my heart for sexual deviants surprisingly vacillates between compassionate sadness for sinners whose sexual norm seems beyond reckoning and repentance without Jesus Christ and absolute hatred of the enemy's twisted work wreaked upon humanity through sexual sin. Hell is a miserable place of unquenchable fire and eternal suffering; how can we snatch people from demon-infested, brimstone pits to offer hope of forgiveness and redemption except through the power of the cross?

While most of my abusers are dead or don't have the power to hurt me anymore, occasionally I've wondered what cocktail of circumstantial chemistry creates monsters from once-innocent kids.

Close your eyes and imagine the time before our shattering. We were all children running in backyards chasing butterflies or climbing trees long before being wrecked or riddled with pain, saddled and broken with self-doubt, searching for self-worth. Before becoming the bully or school shooter fighting for twisted personal power or demonstrating mastery and strength using words, fists, or AK-47s . . . Before the narcissist became self-absorbed in survival or manipulation and demanded the world be brought to her feet at others' expense . . . Before the child molester learned about being groomed . . . They, like you and me, were once kids running around blowing bubbles in the backyard, too, shrieking with delight at each satisfying *pop!* and watching in wonderment as the halos of light floated upward into the yawning sky.

When we become as little children, Jesus says we can come to Him.

Through Holy Spirit–empowered forgiveness, pleading for their salvation in the throne room of God, I've prayed my abusers choose the gospel's saving message of Christ as Lord and Savior before their last breath on earth.

Forgiving those who had a hand creating shattered Little Me has been a process, but I'm doing the best I can. It helps restore the soul of the girl whose only outlet was throwing rocks at farmhouse windows to exert her anger, rage, and power. I especially pray for my mom to know the healing peace of Jesus Christ, but right now, I still haven't been able to face her in person. Not just yet.

As I've desperately mourned, longing for our former mother-daughter interactions, what I've learned is healthy boundaries change the dysfunctional dynamics of emotional and spiritual power. My rage still ebbs and flows alongside sadness and loss as I wonder why and how this happened under her watch.

My King is a miracle-making, restoration-giving Father who gives good and perfect gifts, "who does not change like shifting shadows" and "chose to give us birth through the word of truth, that we might be a kind of firstfruits of all he created" (James 1:17, 18).

Lord, I offer my firstfruits—myself, my life, and my testimony. Reconcile and restore what's broken. Jesus, thank you for being my Immanuel—God with us—now and forever more. Amen.

What Would You Give Up for Lent? My Hands Around Her Throat

3

"What's the chink in your armor? You're a mighty warrior, but what's the door or gate you've left open for enemy access?"

Ash Wednesday 2022. These questions hung in the air seven floors above the street-level din of busy cars and other city sounds. I inhaled deeply, considering them. Steam from sweet milky tea wafted to my nose in tendrils from the mug beside me—a comforting, familiar smell.

"My mother. I haven't fully forgiven her." The answer came surprisingly easy on my exhale, completely without thought and out of my mouth before I could even blink.

"Prayer Warrior Peter" let me sit with my revelation as my friend Chantal silently, prayerfully, continually created space for this healing conversation in her living room. Peter began to pray.

Three years of intense EMDR therapy and counseling finally connected my anxiety, depression, suicidal tendencies, and eating disorders through fractured childhood memories of grooming and abuse trauma. Though I had recorded the journey, done the hard work of healing, and reconciled it biblically, and while I had opened the door for conversation with her, I had not physically faced or confronted the one who may have allowed it to happen . . . my mom.

Though I had forgiven outwardly—stated it aloud, proclaimed it to others, written about it, attempted owning it biblically, spoke to her, and supported her kindly—I still harbored anger and malice in the deep recesses of my hardened heart, feeling justified in holding on to it because I endured heinous, punishable-by-law crimes.

Can we get real here? Can this be a safe space without judgment?

Each time I thought about physically being in a room with her, I imagined myself murderously grabbing her neck, forcing her against the wall, and choking her until she confessed what she knew or begged forgiveness. All the silent gaps between my unanswered questions to her, the need for knowledge, infuriated me. For the record, I know this is not godly—it's the true state of my flesh.

Others agreed it was justifiable, so I excused my hatred for more than two years. I was divided, duplicitous, and completely unrepentant. What I spoke with my mouth didn't align with my heart. Missing family gatherings, I wouldn't let her visit because I was afraid of what I might do or say or react, or that my reaction would slip sideways again to hurt my family.

Second Corinthians 7:10 says, "Godly sorrow brings repentance that leads to salvation and leaves no regret, but worldly sorrow brings death," and Matthew 15:8–9 (a reference to Isaiah 29:13–14) says, "These people honor me with their lips, but their hearts are far from me. They worship me in vain."

The fridge buzzed cyclically in Chantal's kitchen. As a car alarm blared rhythmically, echoing between the buildings on Dearborn Street below us, I knew the time had come for me to stop "playing Christian" with forgiveness and receive the help God had sent me to do it.

"I thought I'd forgiven," I explained, "but it's not true. This is what I see when I think of her . . ." After I confessed the whole of my ugly secret, Peter asked if we could pray yet again.

He began by describing the brutalization of Jesus at the hands of the Romans, and I saw my own hand on the whip, the thorny crown, nail, and hammer. He continued: Christ at Calvary, His shed blood, His forgiveness from the cross.

I began crying.

"I can't FEEL the forgiveness or get to it. I've tried, but I can't do it myself. I need help!"

The anger and hate had been so tightly bound up in my bones they'd migrated down to the marrow and, like armor, had become an iron shield keeping everything holy out and everything horrible in. The unforgiven hurt, betrayal, and anguish rotted and decayed my spirit from within.

"Leigh, can you take all your pain and trauma and place it in a basket? Will you bring it to Jesus for Him to keep?" Peter gently asked.

I cried harder, saying, "It's not fair; I cannot place more on my Savior than He's already carried for me." Realization washed over me: it was prideful to continue to bear this burden, and to release it required humility; it was 1 Peter 5:6–11 all over again.

Scripture says to cast your cares upon Him; He will sustain you and will not let the righteous be shaken (Psalm 55:22). *Oh, Lord, I trust you! It is for freedom that Christ has set me free.* And at that moment, He wanted me to be free indeed.

Preparing the basket wasn't pretty, but sin never is. Wood and wicker caning groaned under the weight and, mercifully, I didn't have to peek under the dirty linen covering to know everything I was carrying. Trusting Holy Spirit to do the work, I lifted it all to Jesus and the burden dissolved. It seems when we walk bravely with reckless courage and ridiculous obedience, Jesus does His beautiful work. Sobbing from the release, relieved and spiritually light, I found the darkness was gone.

Peter asked about my mom again. "All I see is my arms around her, a full-body hug without reservation.

There's so much love and peace!" We celebrated, praising God for His goodness.

The next morning at 5:00 a.m. Bible study, our leader asked how we see God in Psalm 37. When my turn came, I told the ladies, "He is a liberator!" and offered testimony to encourage them and celebrate again.

Wouldn't you know it—that afternoon, not twenty-four hours after praying with Peter, my phone buzzed.

"Hey, Momma," I answered.

It's Not Always a One-and-Done . . . Until It Is

"We're bringing him home to die."

Mom told me her husband was coming home from the hospital and beginning hospice care. My heart hurt for her. Before we hung up, the Holy Spirit nudged me to reach out and complete the circle.

"I'm sending you a big hug. Can you feel it, Mom?" I asked.

She paused, then responded, her voice cracking, "Yes, I can. Thank you."

He died five days later, in the late afternoon on Tuesday. A Thursday flight from O'Hare brought me to Denver within forty-eight hours of his passing. It had been four or five years since I'd seen her or gone back home.

Triggered and panicking as the rental car carried me past memories and ghosts long dead down I-25 and into town, I fought against the darkness that was trying to wiggle its way through my armor. It was aching to overtake me; I refused to let it gain ground. Easing the car onto the shoulder, I prayed and texted friends for prayer coverage. My voice shaking, I spoke aloud. "In the name of Jesus, I rebuke you. I stand in victory!"

And I did . . . because Christ did.

No power in hell separates us from the love of God that is in Jesus Christ. That day, the enemy lost his grip on me. I knew I was wrapped in the loving arms of the Father, that there was now no condemnation, that I was free from sin and death to serve unreservedly with loving boundaries (Romans 8:1–2, 31–39). So I walked through the door of the house that was once filled with the stench of death and ghosts of abusers past to become the fragrance of Christ the best way I knew how.

In His goodness and mercy, God showed me ways to open-handedly honor my mother in one of her greatest times of need by doing the job I was sent to do. There was a lot of wholehearted hugging and hand-holding. We wrote his obituary together, which was a cathartic release for me and healing for her. She asked me to sing at the gravesite, but I kindly refused and offered other suggestions because I didn't know if she knew how singing triggered me in this context. Mom shared the hardships of the past months tending her husband through dementia and illness and, finally, as his earthly body failed. We shared a tender time: I pray she felt heard, supported, and loved because that was the job the Lord sent me to do.

Hours before leaving, I felt God prompting me to explain why I hadn't seen her for so many years. Finding the strength and courage to finally confront her face-to-face, I simply said, "I have been really angry and upset with you."

Without inquiring or asking for a single detail, she stood silently with her mouth open, the doorway framing her like a live, unblinking portrait. For the first time, she understood I knew everything she allowed to happen to me as a tiny girl at the hands of the men she brought into our home.

Tension hung between us like an iron weight. She wasn't going to try to make it right because she didn't have the tools to try.

And that's OK. Because my Savior healed my hurts and took away the pain, I could love Mom right where she was for who she was without receiving apology or explanation—loving the sinner, hating the sin. The longer I waited, the burden of pain shifted from my shoulders onto hers. I looked into her eyes with compassion and pity and spoke these words:

"All is forgiven; there is forgiveness, Mom."

When we own our own stories, we avoid being trapped as characters in stories someone else is telling.

—Brené Brown, *Rising Strong*

In the end, we will individually account for our lives, words, and deeds before the throne of the Most High on judgment day. As much as we forgive others, even when it means forgiving the same offense again and again, not seven times but seven times seventy-seven times (that's 539 times!), we are measured by our own standards. That scares me sometimes if I think about it too much. "For we know him who said, 'Vengeance is mine; I will repay.' And again, 'The Lord will judge His people.' It is a fearful thing to fall into the hands of the living God" (Hebrews 10:30–31 ESV).

My part is trusting in Jesus and being intentionally obedient to do the work placed before me. God's part is healing and making me whole, reconciling the past and restoring my life, now and eternally.

What's the chink in your armor?

Peter's question haunts me.

Ever wonder if there's earthly freedom with certain issues or if we're consigned to suffer until heavenly perfection? I have. I've wondered, *Are my thorns left embedded to keep me humble as I constantly search for His grace that's sufficient, His power made perfect in my weakness?* Had unforgiveness held back my healing and allowed the darkness to overcome me?

"Father, forgive them, for they know not what they are doing," Jesus proclaimed at Calvary as he took my place on the cross that was meant for me (Luke 23:34). He died for me to live; His life ransomed mine because He bridged the gap for my sin. Forgiveness is the key to the kingdom . . . then and now.

Praise you, Lord Jesus. It is finished.

How great Thou art.

Verses to Consider

Isaiah 29:13–14
Matthew 15:8–9
2 Corinthians 7:10

She Seems So Normal podcast

Epilogue

THE PLASTIC PRINCESS DECONSTRUCTED (OR, LIVING AUTHENTIC, MESSY FAITH)

It's February 2022, and let's be honest, the last time I intentionally wrote about my journey in late December 2020, I thought I would be completely healed and headed for a "normal" life without issues or panic attacks or . . . whatever. While I recognize I've made huge strides discovering the root causes and managing childhood sexual abuse (CSA) trauma symptoms, sometimes it's like trying to rinse a bucket that was formerly filled with concrete: no matter how long you clean, a stubborn, gritty residue always clings to scratches on the surface. You gotta just keep wiping.

Initially, when I decided to publish this narrative, though I received multiple well-timed, godly confirmations, the terror nearly eclipsed the excitement. The fear barrier is so real for trauma survivors that, when triggered, we respond as if we're in jeopardy of physical harm even when we're miles or decades from initial causes.

My body impulsively began reliving trauma symptoms at wonky times throughout the following week. An

all-out panic attack in the afternoon. Terrifying nightmares. Obsessive behavior for my family's safety. Body
shaming by compulsive criticism, hateful thoughts about
my appearance. The desperate need to numb, dissociate,
or distract.

The enemy of my soul is not creative. The same scare
tactic tricks previously plaguing me resurfaced. But give
praise to Jesus because this time I knew better and managed
more efficiently by calling on the coping resources and the
network God provided over these last months.

Isn't it funny?

As a new Christian, I used to want everyone to
think I had my ish together, that my world was practically perfect in every way. Acting and dressing as what I
thought was the ideal Christian woman, projecting the
ideal marriage and family and ministry, I now realize
that whenever I looked in the mirror, I never actually
faced the real me, the one who Jesus fearfully, wonderfully created, a woman He loves all the way to hell and
back up to heaven. What I saw back then was a plastic
princess, a "church girl" mannequin. Whenever that
plastic-princess facade melted offscreen under pressure,
I remolded and remodeled her again and again, wondering why I felt like such a fraud, an impostor of faith.

Now I know why.

That filtered, formulated girl was never authentically
me. She was just what I thought others wanted or
needed. Even with her best intentions, that plastic
princess/church girl was a manufactured, devil-distorted
caricature, a mere shadowy outline of the woman God
created me to be.

Honest accountability and the willingness to be vulnerable with safe, biblically minded people—coupled with humility to be openly teachable to loving critical feedback—are my keys to finding freedom to love and accept my true self, flaws and all. Shame will no longer silence or keep me from help.

Joan Rivers said, "I wish I could tell you it gets better, but it doesn't get better. YOU get better."[1] Though she was encouraging another comedian not to abandon the craft, the quote applies to trauma recovery.

Don't quit. Stay the course. Add to what you already have. For us as Christians, that's goodness, knowledge, self-control, perseverance, godliness, mutual affection, and love to our existing faith (2 Peter 1:5–7). Encourage those who run through the same valley of the shadow of death. Maybe most importantly for us, make Jesus known among the nations and proclaim His wonderful works (Psalm 105:1–2).

I wish I could tell you this story's a one-and-done, but it's not; there's still more God's rewriting in my heart, mind, body, and spirit. I wish I could report my life is perfectly reconstructed, but that would be a plastic-princess lie because I'm still running through deep gorges, still struggling at times. At least it's honest, and recognizing the work ahead to remain healthy, by God's grace, I've already progressed so far so fast.

Perhaps from this earthly side of the cross, I'll carry thorns reminding me of my weaknesses, like the apostle Paul, never achieving complete emotional or physical healing or wholeness, but until I'm enraptured by my Lord and Savior face-to-face, I'll have faith His grace is sufficient and perfectly powerful for fighting to live in God's truth with every last breath in my body. The battle is worth waging through every gorge and wasteland because those waiting with Jesus at the heavenly finish line might not only be my husband, children, or friends but possibly generations blessed by a single woman's obedient willingness to forgive her abusers and place her absolute trust in Christ to reconcile, restore, and redeem beauty from ashes and break sinful cycles of death here on earth.

There is power in the name of Jesus

To BREAK every chain, break EVERY chain,
break every CHAIN.[2]

She Seems So Normal podcast

Listen to "Break Every Chain"

You prepare a table before me in the presence
of my enemies;
You have anointed my head with oil;
My cup overflows.
Surely goodness and lovingkindness will follow me
all the days of my life,
And I will dwell in the house of the L<small>ORD</small> *forever.*

—Psalm 23:5–6 (NASB1995)

NOTES

Introduction: The Shattering

1. Opening *Redeeming Heartache: How Past Suffering Reveals Our True Calling* by Dr. Dan B. Allender and Cathy Loerzel (Grand Rapids, MI: Zondervan, 2022) to part 1, titled "The Shattering," which describes trauma's chemical, emotional, and relational dysregulation from a professional counseling angle, I was amazed how closely Allender's technical explanation mirrored my personal narrative and that both manuscripts were composed at the same time during the pandemic.

1. The Hardest Story I Never Shared

1. Brené Brown, "Shame vs. Guilt," *Brené Brown* (blog), January 15, 2013, https://brenebrown.com/articles/2013/01/15/shame-v-guilt.
2. "What Is Learned Helplessness?," Medical News Today, accessed May 31, 2019, https://www.medicalnewstoday.com/articles/325355#summary.
3. Brandon O'Connor, "The Army Is Changing: Current Female Cadets Will Enter the Army with More Career Options than Ever," US Army, June 10, 2020, https://www.army.mil/article/236362/the_army_is_changing_current_female_cadets_will_enter_the_army_with_more_career_options_than_ever.
4. Karoun Demirjian, "Reported Sexual Assault Cases Climb at Military Academies Despite Prevention Efforts," *Washington Post*, February 17, 2022, https://www.washingtonpost.com/national-security/2022/02/17/military-academies-sex-assault/.
5. I do not capitalize any names for satan and explain this in chapter 6.

2. Systematic Grooming Normalizes Abuse

1. "Grooming," National Society for the Prevention of Cruelty to Children, accessed July 20, 2022, https://www.nspcc.org .uk/what-is-child-abuse/types-of-abuse/grooming.
2. Marc Lacey and Jonathan Kandell, "A Last Vanishing Act for Robert Vesco, Fugitive," *New York Times*, May 3, 2008, https:// www.nytimes.com/2008/05/03/world/americas/03vesco .html; "Robert L. Vesco," *Britannica*, last updated November 30, 2021, https://www.britannica.com/biography /Robert-L-Vesco.
3. Here is one resource: Kristen A. Jenson, "#MeToo—10 Ways Predators Are Grooming Kids," October 26, 2017, https://www.defendyoungminds.com/post/10-ways -predators-grooming-kids.

3. Testing God, Tough Questions

1. Dr. Dan B. Allender's book *The Wounded Heart: Hope for Adult Victims of Childhood Sexual Abuse* (Colorado Springs: NavPress, 1990) was the best Christian book I read that biblically detailed the medical, psychological, and spiritual aspects of reconciling my experiences to offer hope for healing. Since it had such impactful explanations, I asked my husband to read it.
2. A great resource to help here is Timothy Keller, *The Reason for God: Belief in an Age of Skepticism* (New York: Riverhead Books, 2008).
3. Various dates documenting where I was on my journey are noted throughout the book and are formatted MM.DD.YYYY.
4. C. S. Lewis, *The Great Divorce* in *The Complete C. S. Lewis Signature Classics* (New York: HarperOne, 2022), 519.

4. On the Lookout for Wise Counsel

1. A great resource for codependency is Melody Beattie, *Codependent No More: How to Stop Controlling Others and Start Caring for Yourself* (Center City, MN: Hazelden, 1986).
2. John Wesley, *A Plain Account of Christian Perfection* (Peabody, MA: Hendrickson, 2007), 117.

6. Is Mental Health the New Leprosy in Church?

1. Susan Roberts, "Mental Illness in the Church—What You Need to Know," Care Net, June 20, 2018, https://www.care-net.org/churches-blog/mental-illness-how-can-you-help.
2. "13 Stats on Mental Health and the Church," Lifeway Research, May 1, 2018, https://research.lifeway.com/2018/05/01/13-stats-on-mental-health-and-the-church/.
3. "What Is EMDR?," EMDR Institute, accessed July 20, 2022, https://www.emdr.com/what-is-emdr/.
4. For more about post-traumatic stress disorder (PTSD), visit the National Center for PTSD at https://www.ptsd.va.gov/.
5. The name "d'Evil" is my term for our adversary, the accuser, whom the Bible calls satan, the serpent, and the devil. Spelling it "d'Evil" points out the evil that he personifies. I refuse beginning any names for him with a capital to imply a proper noun because there's nothing proper about evil.

7. Baklava Day and Boxed-Up Memories

1. Frank Sonnenberg, "The Power to Forgive," The Robert D. and Billie Ray Center at Drake University, December 12, 2016, https://raycenter.wp.drake.edu/2016/12/12/the-power-to-forgive/#:~:text=Smedes%2C%20the%20renowned%20theologian%2C%20said,resentment%20and%20thoughts%20of%20revenge.

9. Origin of My Shattering

1. My word *ish* is a friendlier, non-swearing term for *$h1+*.
2. Anne Walther, "What Is Wabi Sabi? The Elusive Beauty of Imperfection," Japan Objects, January 8, 2021, https://japanobjects.com/features/wabi-sabi.

10. Restoring Identity

1. Check out the video on YouTube: Dr. Edward Tronick, "Still Face Experiment," March 25, 2016, YouTube video, 2:48, https://www.youtube.com/watch?v=YTTSXc6sARg.

12. Warping the Image of God

1. Body dysmorphic disorder (BDD) often begins in adolescence as an extreme focus on perceived physical flaws, causing severe emotional distress and difficulties in daily functioning. According to the Anxiety and Depression Association of America, BDD affects one in fifty people in the United States. For more information on treating BDD, please see "Understanding Body Dysmorphic Disorder," Anxiety and Depression Association of America, https://adaa.org/understanding-anxiety/body-dysmorphic-disorder and "Body Dysmorphic Disorder," Johns Hopkins Medicine, https://www.hopkinsmedicine.org/health/conditions-and-diseases/body-dysmorphic-disorder.
2. Brené Brown, *Dare to Lead* (New York: Random House, 2018), 257.

14. Healing Ain't All Champagne and Caviar Dreams

1. "Amanda," on Waylon Jennings, *The Ramblin' Man*, RCA Victor, 1974.

15. Lesson One: God Sees Beauty in Our Brokenness

1. Mark I. Bubeck, *Warfare Praying: Biblical Strategies for Overcoming the Adversary* (Chicago: Moody, 2016), 26.
2. Deuteronomy 6:4–9; Matthew 22:37; Mark 12:30; Luke 10:27.

16. Lesson Two: Avoid Isolation—It's Dark and Dangerous

1. Francine Rivers, comment on Leigh Mackenzie, *The Church Girl Writes* (blog), https://leighmackenzie.com/desole-writing-through-the-honest-powerful-emotions-of-suicidal-hopelessness-and-coming-out-the-other-side-stronger/.

17. Lesson Three: Tools of the Trauma Trade—God Is Enough/God's Toolbox

1. "Anxiety Disorders—Facts & Statistics," Anxiety and Depression Association of America, accessed July 20, 2022, https://adaa.org/understanding-anxiety/facts-statistics.

2. Tim Newman, "Anxiety in the West: Is it on the Rise?," Medical News Today, September 5, 2018, https://www.medical newstoday.com/articles/322877.

3. Not gonna lie, if you know the GDP of Ethiopia you get a prize, but if you've memorized more than your family's social security numbers, you're getting a fish-eye!

4. While you're grooving, check out the wonders of EFT tapping and bilateral stimulation online.

19. Lesson Five: Develop Vulnerability, Cultivate Courage

1. Brené Brown, *The Gifts of Imperfection* (Swift Books, 2020).

2. To learn more about Jesus as Lord and Savior, check out https://thestoryfilm.com and https://movingworks.org.

3. Brené Brown, *Rising Strong: How the Ability to Reset Transforms the Way We Live, Love, Parent, and Lead* (New York: Random House, 2015), xix.

21. Lesson Seven: Sacred Spheres of Support

1. Brené Brown, *Daring Greatly: How the Courage to Be Vulnerable Transforms the Way We Live, Love, Parent, and Lead* (New York: Avery, 2012), 58.

2. See John Townsend and Henry Cloud, *Boundaries: When to Say Yes, How to Say No to Take Control of Your Life* (Grand Rapids, MI: Zondervan, 2017).

3. For real. Zebras en masse are called "dazzles" or "zeals." A group of hippos is called a "bloat," but my favorite animal herd description is the rhino: "crash." See "A Smack of Jellyfish, a Zeal of Zebras, and Other Fun Animal Group Names," Dictionary.com, March 3, 2021, https://www.dictionary .com/e/strange-animal-groups-listicle/.

4. Check out Jeanne's book, *What's Here Now? How to Stop Rehashing the Past and Rehearsing the Future—and Start Receiving the Present* (Grand Rapids, MI: Revell, 2022).

5. I am referring to the New International Version of the Bible. Other translations use it even more. The Message uses it fifty times; the New Living Translation, sixty-two; The New

American Standard Bible 1995, sixty-seven; and the New
King James Version, seventy-five.
6. See the *Hebrew-Greek Key Word Study Bible*, NIV (Chattanooga:
AMG International, 1996). If you would like to read more
about this Hebrew word and delve into its multilayered meaning, visit https://www.blueletterbible.org/lexicon/h3365
/web/wlc/0-1/.

22. Lesson Eight: Forgiveness Is the Key to the Kingdom

1. C. S. Lewis, *The Great Divorce* in *The Complete C. S. Lewis Signature
Classics* (New York: HarperOne, 2022), 465–66.

Epilogue: The Plastic Princess Deconstructed (Or, Living Authentic, Messy Faith)

1. Samantha Grossman, "Hear the Wise Words Joan Rivers
Said on *Louie* About Being a Comedian," *Time*, September 4,
2014, https://time.com/3270472/joan-rivers-dead-louie/.
It's ironic that Joan said this on a show hosted by a comedian
who fell from grace in the wake of the #MeToo movement
and now I'm using it to empower survivors. I think it shows
that survivors can take inspiration from anywhere and own it.
2. "Break Every Chain," by Will Reagan and Jennie Lee Riddle,
track 4 on Jesus Culture, *Awakening—Live from Chicago*, Jesus
Culture Music, 2011. The emphasis on the words is mine.

ABOUT THE AUTHOR

For three years as a sermon research assistant at one of the first multisite megachurches, Leigh Mackenzie shared her love and talent for delving deeply into Scripture to extract biblical truths and original perspectives on teaching and personal application for her preaching team.

Known as "The Church Girl Writes" on social media and as one of Pureflix's Top Christian Mommy Bloggers in 2019, Leigh has written articles for *Hobby Farms Chickens* magazine and regularly appeared in *Christian Standard* magazine writing on subjects from child trafficking to thrift-store ministry.

Her Bible study questions for *The Lookout* magazine, one of the nation's oldest Bible study guides for adults, and online communion meditations for *Christian Standard* have equipped Restoration Movement laypeople and leaders for ministry. She has also written devotional material for *The Upper Room*.

Leigh can be heard narrating parts of her story on the *She Seems So Normal* podcast and reflecting on her own trauma-healing journey shattering the Plastic Princess to embrace authentic faith and interviewing other key players you met throughout this book.

Married thirty years to her beloved West Pointer, Leigh and Christopher are both passionate about future ministry opportunities and exploring God's world together.

Connect with Leigh!

If you enjoyed this book, will you consider sharing the message with others?

Let us know your thoughts. You can let the author know by visiting or sharing a photo of the cover on our social media pages or leaving a review at a retailer's site. All of it helps us get the message out!

Email: info@ironstreammedia.com

  @ironstreammedia

Iron Stream, Iron Stream Fiction, Iron Stream Kids, Brookstone Publishing Group, and Life Bible Study are imprints of Iron Stream Media, which derives its name from Proverbs 27:17, "As iron sharpens iron, so one person sharpens another." This sharpening describes the process of discipleship, one to another. With this in mind, Iron Stream Media provides a variety of solutions for churches, ministry leaders, and nonprofits ranging from in-depth Bible study curriculum and Christian book publishing to custom publishing and consultative services.

For more information on ISM and its imprints, please visit IronStreamMedia.com

Made in the USA
Monee, IL
11 November 2022

17529121R00144